Printed in the United States of America

First Printing, 2024

ISBN: 979-8-3303-3565-7

EliciaN@gmail.com
Scottsdale, AZ 85258

Back Cover image: Inês Piquet Images

First Edition

"Grief is the cost of loving."[1]

-Dr. Glennon Doyle

---

[1] This quote is drawn from the book Untamed, published in 2020 by prominent author and activist Dr. Glennon Doyle.

Don't Be A Stranger To Grief

Healing through Letters
Connecting Pain to Purpose

Elicia Nademin, PhD, ABPP

Don't Be A Stranger To Grief

Healing Through Letters Connecting Pain to Purpose

Dedication

This book is dedicated to my mother, Farideh, my beloved late father, Ali, and my forever baby, Kaylie. Today, Kaylie is 16 years old! While she still looks like a puppy, my heart aches as I watch the aging process happen. Kaylie baby, I continue to cherish every moment with you. I can only hope that the joy and sweetness you emanate every day reflect the love you feel from me.

To my father, you are forever in my thoughts. Until the day I die, I will strive to be as kind and honorable as you were until you took your last breath. You remain my inspiration for my every crazy whim. To my mother, you've inspired in me the strength and courage to confront fear and to live a life I'm proud of. You've taught me to live life in a way that drives joy, acceptance, and alignment with my moral compass. Let's continue to breathe beauty into the moments and lead with love and light.

My first book, *Don't Be A Stranger,* on fostering more memorable first impressions and connections with strangers, was meant to fulfill my father's wish to have his daughter publish. This book is for the general public and honors my clients. Selfishly, it also satisfies my wish of leaving the world a little better than I found it. In *Don't Be A Stranger To Grief,* I introduce you to an intervention I designed in session with a client one day many years ago. My hope is to make this exercise widely accessible in hopes that it may help others whom I may never have the privilege of meeting.

I could not have felt inspired to write *Don't Be A Stranger To Grief* if not for repeatedly sitting in awe of clients I've served as we navigated through journeys with grief. My sincerest gratitude goes to every client (and friend) who has trusted me in their most intimate moments of pain. I am grateful for the consent to share their thoughts, feelings, and writings with you as a model for healing. While names and personal information have been de-identified, you know who you are. Your courage is admirable, and your words are impactful! I hope you take comfort in knowing your journey helps pave the way for others. There is no right way to grieve. There is simply movement. There is acceptance. There is surrender. There is peace in recognizing the gift of what was and what may come of it.

While I recognize that one book will not eradicate pain and that bereavement is a fluid process, I wish to be a source of light and support along your journey. If even one person finds comfort in this work, my wish will have been granted.

Table of Contents

Foreword

*H*ow do you find purpose and joy after tragedy? A client and I recently examined this question. When I experience difficult times, my best friend Brookie reminds me: "Lise, this will be purposed for your highest good." I offered this perspective to my client. He found great comfort in considering that ***how*** he would overcome a tragedy might serve his highest good in his remaining years with loved ones. We could not know when or how, but we shared faith that it would.

As Viktor Frankl (1984) wrote in his book *Man's Search for Meaning* a person is less likely to survive if they view their suffering as meaningless. Regardless of circumstance, we always possess the freedom to choose our response. Discovering purpose fuels survival and propels us to pursue a life we look forward to living. Sometimes, this can be as fundamental as upholding hope that the coming days will bring ease and connection.

Regardless of your faith, I hope you find comfort, peace, and solace in the writings herein. This brief work introduces you to an intervention I call the *Release With Love Letter*. For years, I have applied the *Release With Love Letter* technique with clients in my psychology practice. In so doing, I have witnessed profound healing across countless clients—each has astonished me. The intervention, though simple, possesses remarkable potency. Through this book, I aim to make the *Release With Love Letter* template easily accessible to the public. I hope to help you apply this tool to cultivate peace and purpose in your healing journeys.

Who might benefit from writing a *Release With Love Letter*? I'd argue anyone. The *Release With Love Letter* can be applied to soothe feelings around longing, loss, trauma, and regret. A *Release With Love Letter* may be written to yourself or addressed to another person. It can be used to manage feelings around the loss of dreams or a life plan that has gone unmet. You might write a *Release With Love Letter* if you find it hard to let go of someone who has passed or left your life in any way. Maybe you want them back, maybe you don't. You might write a *Release With Love Letter* if you feel haunted by regrets or avoid thoughts of someone who's gone.

Lingering unease, avoidance, or guardedness when thinking of a loss may be evidence of unresolved grief. These can show as "I don't want to's" or other indicators of resistance to broaching the subject of a loss. I believe that everyone you meet, you meet for a reason. Some teach you how you want to be; others bring clarity to traits, habits, mannerisms, and other features that you choose to resist. May we learn to accept, embrace, and detach with love.

Learning to release pain and grief-related feelings will be a gradual process. Healing will likely manifest as a softening of intense feelings moreso than an absence of emotional charge. Releasing is not forgetting. Please consider that a *Release With Love Letter* is not a substitute for professional help. I might even suggest you conduct the exercise and review your letter with a therapist or grief professional to facilitate your healing process. **To mental health providers and helping professionals wishing to direct clients to the *Release With Love Letter* template, please refer to a) *Appendix C* for *Note to Clinicians & Helping Professionals* and b) *Appendix D* for an overview of *Grief Management Resources.***

As you proceed in learning how to *Release With Love,* please consider the words of 13th-century Persian poet Jalaluddin Rumi in his famous poem *The Guest House (1995) as translated by Coleman Barks:*

> This being human is a guest house.
> Every morning a new arrival.
>
> A joy, a depression, a meanness,
> some momentary awareness comes
> as an unexpected visitor.
>
> Welcome and entertain them all!
> Even if they're a crowd of sorrows,
> who violently sweep your house
> empty of its furniture,
> still, treat each guest honorably.
> He may be clearing you out
> for some new delight.
>
> The dark thought, the shame, the malice,
> meet them at the door laughing,
> and invite them in.
>
> Be grateful for whoever comes,
> because each has been sent
> as a guide from beyond.

This poem represents an examination, welcoming, and acceptance of all emotions and experiences that are part of the human condition. My father used to say, "Elish, in our culture, even if our enemy were to show up at the door, we are to welcome them in and offer them tea." I see this poem as a metaphoric extension of my father's words.

Rumi suggests that each emotion guides us to remain open and receptive to lessons. Readers are encouraged to welcome all feelings as wise guests and to engage with them. The poem likens humanness to a guest house, relating all emotions, good and bad, as unexpected visitors who come and go, each carrying a message. It is our responsibility and privilege to listen. The underlying message is to trust the inherent wisdom and spiritual order of the universe. *The Guest House* speaks to the importance of grace, growth, and surrender. The reader is prompted to embrace a profound level of self-awareness and acceptance. Rumi so gracefully speaks to the impermanence and importance of emotions and the fluid nature of life.

Remember Rumi's words as you welcome all emerging emotions during the *Release With Love* exercise that follows. Each feeling is a reminder of a season that will have served your highest good. You may not know how or when but believe it to be true. Even if you're wrong, you'll have suffered less. You will feel more hopeful for upholding faith that there will have been purpose in your pain, and hope feeds purpose to get to another day. Let's make meaning of shared moments, joyful and painful, in a way that is touching, honoring, and inspiring as you navigate life in your coming years.

Chapter 1:
Why Release With Love?

*W*hy learn to *Release With Love*? Simple, to have peace and to feel you are living a life of purpose. *Release With Love* to recognize your pain as not wasted. *Release With Love* to interact with the world with greater kindness and gentleness. *Release With Love* to lead with light.

The *Release With Love Letter* template is designed to help you acknowledge hurt and grief as reminders of a wish you once had and perhaps still do. Allow your letter to inspire steps toward fostering meaningful relationships and a purpose-driven life. Your wish still may come true, simply by way of a path you had not planned for. I have avoided reference to research or technical concepts in this text. While credentialed as a board-certified behavioral and cognitive psychologist, I consider myself an empath.

As an empathic healer, I support my clients intuitively. I listen deeply and draw on innate abilities to trust, know, and heal. I develop interventions instinctively based on what is present at the moment. Intuition has been defined by *Psychology Today* as a faculty in which hunches are generated by the unconscious mind rapidly sifting through past experience and cumulative knowledge (Verny, 2023).

The gift of inner knowing is present in all of us to varying degrees. I apply my gift to the therapeutic process, collaboratively guiding clients through interventions underpinned by the science and research of psychology, theory, and principles of interpersonal therapies.

I created the *Release With Love Letter* spontaneously years ago while in session with a veteran who was struggling with unresolved grief. He had lost a dear friend and was haunted by many regrets about things he wished he had said, had done, and time he wished he could get back. One day, I asked if this client would humor me. He agreed as we experimented with a new intervention. I intuitively guided him through prompts to complete several feelings-oriented statements to help him *feel* deeper. I hoped this would allow us to capture and organize his feelings, regrets, wishes, and commitments in honoring memories of his late friend. I had no expectation of what would come of this exercise.

I have often found that the most extraordinary blessings in life come in unexpected packages. The spontaneous creativity my client and I engaged that day is the basis for the book you are now reading. In completing this exercise, my client identified long-suppressed feelings and long-held regrets he'd been afraid to voice. Most profoundly, he recognized that much of his suffering was around not having reached out more to his friend before he died. He reflected on ways he could meaningfully honor the bond they shared. My client did so in a way that drew laughter as he reminisced on lighter, playful moments of their friendship.

By the end of that inaugural writing of the *Release With Love Letter*, my client had teared up; he had laughed; in the end, he breathed more deeply. When I read his writing back to him, he expressed deep comfort and relief. He felt lighter. It seemed he gave himself permission to laugh again. He committed to keeping alive the humor he and his friend shared.

It is worth mentioning that after we completed the *Release With Love Letter* that day, my client and I discussed how he might further memorialize the memory of his friend and honor what he'd created. He told me weeks later that he made himself copies of the letter. He shared one copy with his late friend's wife. He scheduled a beautiful ceremony with friends to honor his late friend's memory. He read his letter aloud at the ceremony. He later read the letter aloud to himself once again before destroying and releasing it with love.

In the weeks and months that followed the exercise my client completed, he took steps toward honoring his commitment to reach out more to family and friends. He'd previously resisted doing so because of his outstanding guilt and having labeled himself "a bad friend." As time and treatment went on, his depression lifted, anxiety of unaddressed regrets improved, and his perceived sense of 'badness' resolved. He was surprised as he started to see his positive impact on the lives around him.

Unfortunately, I don't have a copy of that first *Release With Love Letter*. I never could have imagined the power it would carry in the years to follow. I wonder if my client will ever know the influence his willingness to experiment with me has had on the lives of so many people after him. I am grateful to that brave man for co-creating the space in which the *Release With Love Letter* was born.

Since witnessing the magnitude of relief my client felt after writing the first ever *Release With Love Letter*, I've adapted this exercise with countless other clients. *Release With Love Letters* have been helpful in treatment with many of our nation's veterans, young and old, who have experienced immense and tragic loss. The exercise has been adapted to support clients overcoming depression and anxiety and those facing serious medical illness including amputation and end-of-life conditions. I've adapted *Release With Love Letters* among those undergoing relational loss including divorce, breakup, or major moves and job changes. Letters have been comforting for those embracing evolution around identity and sexuality. I've even found great value in applying the intervention with entrepreneurs and partners in my anti-aging business as we uncover barriers to success, such as fear of failure and judgment frequently rooted in memories of self-doubt or criticism.

So often, we ache in missing what is gone. Yet, we shy away from discussing our feelings due to fear of being engulfed by sadness, anger, regret, and other complex reactions tied to our loss. These common reactions to loss are encapsulated in the seminal Kübler-Ross (1969) Five Stages of Grief model, which describes how individuals facing loss tend to cycle through stages of denial, anger, bargaining, depression, and acceptance while navigating the grieving process. These stages are not necessarily sequential and may be revisited. Each accompanying emotion plays an essential role in your healing.

You may worry about how others will respond and support you in your pain. This intervention is designed to be simple enough to be carried out at home alone, but it is generally most effective when completed with the support of a friend, therapist, mentor, coach, or other partner along your journey of healing and self-care. I applaud you for your willingness to confront your grief.

As James Baldwin said,

> *"Not everything that is faced can be changed,*
> *but nothing can be changed until it is faced."*

People are so uniquely different, so each *Release With Love Letter* is adapted to fit a client's unique pattern of grief. In the ensuing pages, I have included letters from diverse clients and friends so you may have a deeper understanding of how to adapt the *Release With Love Letter* template to honor your unique reality. I obtained the permission of each client, friend, and my very own beloved mother to include their writings herein.

Release With Love Letters are often met with tremendous relief, healthy promotion of grief processing, healing, and gratitude for truths revealed.

Typical responses in completing the practice are tears followed simply by, "Wow." I interpret these responses as symbolic of a release of emotions and wisdom that people don't always realize they carry intrinsically.

As you write, consider the role of anger. Anger can be difficult to acknowledge, yet it is so important. As my dear friend and beloved psychologist Dr. Jon McCaine wrote in *Moments of Truth* (2022), "Anger is love disappointed." Allow yourself to feel anger in recalling parts you once loved and still desire, as a means to gauge fulfillment in future relationships.

Sadly, some feel that life is no longer worth living after loss. We may feel guilty smiling or laughing as though this would detract from the significance of those lost. We may be grieving a life we had envisioned, a marriage, a child, a parent, a sibling, a friend, a breakup, or an identity that is entirely different than previously imagined. I'm here to remind you that life still has a purpose, and you are still very much wanted and needed. Those no longer with us live on *through us* in the legacies they leave behind. We get to decide in part what that legacy means for us, and our lives can change tremendously from that decision.

One of my favorite depictions of the power of perspective is that of a turtle on its back. I published this little one in my first book, *Don't Be a Stranger: Creating Connections & Memorable First Impressions in Everyday Life.* You might pity the turtle, thinking it's stuck in place, immobile,

paralyzed. However, as you see in the image, the turtle may feel as free as a bird, glaring up at the beautiful blue sky. Pain is about perspective.

Losing my father was the most brutal loss I've lived through, though I wouldn't give back that pain. The pain I experience in grieving his loss is a measure of how deeply I got to feel his love. I experienced the love of an incredible man whose presence will forever be a gift that lives on through me in perspective, empathy, and gratitude toward others. That said, I wouldn't function well if I were chronically buried in my grief. I've turned my pain into purpose.

In the years since losing my father, I have sought new ways to honor him. I honor my father daily through my work as a Psychologist and advocate for elderly and vulnerable clients. Truth be told, many of my older guys remind me of him, and I feel like I get to give them the care I would have wanted for my father in his most tender days. I honor my father when I treat fellow humans with compassion and kindness. I honor my father when I engage my visionary spirit. I honor him when I think before I speak. I honor him when I practice patience in my life.

What about if the person gone was not a positive influence or a source of kindness in your life? What if they were a source of constant pain or hurt? Perhaps even violence? I would offer you the same advice: seek purpose in your pain. Perhaps you'll consider the person lost as a model you'll strive *never* to emulate. Consider how you *want* to leave people feeling. Perhaps you'll serve as an advocate for others or develop self-compassion along your healing journey. Perhaps you'll reclaim (or claim) inner resilience, reminding yourself of your power within as a survivor...the power that no one gets to take away from you.

However you navigate your grief, you must progress *through* it to heal. The next section will guide you on the *how* of the *Release With Love* process, detailing the sections of the letter and offering recommendations to keep your writing focused, concise, yet impactful.

Chapter 2:
How To Release With Love

The elegant simplicity of this intervention may surprise you. I aimed for this template to be thorough enough to capture the pattern of primary emotions typically associated with grief. It is designed to keep you positively focused, promoting resiliency and connecting purpose to the pain underlying grief. The intention is for anyone going through grief to be able to repeat this exercise on their own, adapting it as their grief transforms over time and with each unique loss. Consider the *Release With Love Letter* an adapted form of journaling that helps to retrain your mindset around loss. The more Release With Love Letters you write, the more you'll habituate the process of directing your pain as a catalyst toward purpose-driven change and healing.

While I am known for my verbosity, I'll let the *Release With Love Letters* and testimonials speak for themselves as I step aside. I have little doubt you'll quickly witness the power of these letters as you read on. I extend heartfelt gratitude to all who have walked this journey with me and to those who have allowed me to share your intimate letters. May others learn and feel inspired by your examples of vulnerability and strength.

One final note. Please be prepared as you may experience strong emotions while writing a Release with Love Letter (RWLL). It can be beneficial to plan to be with a trusted friend, engage in a comforting activity, or practice self-affirmation to help you feel connected and supported after writing your RWLL letter. This will help you stay grounded as you process your feelings fully. And now, without further ado, let's review the core elements of the *Release With Love Letter*.

To Whom Your Letter Is Addressed:

As you prepare to draft your *Release With Love Letter*, start by thinking of who or what you are grieving. Remember, you may write a letter to *yourself,* another person alive or past, a wish, an identity, or a life that is no longer.

Ask For Help, If Available:

The *Release With Love Letter* exercise can be done alone; however, writing one alone may predispose you to get distracted by wanting to edit or correct yourself as you write. I highly recommend asking a trusted confidante (friend, family, lover, therapist, pastor, or other accountability partner you feel emotionally and physically safe with) to help you with this exercise. Dictating your responses rather than writing them out as you think also helps you avoid focusing on sentence structure, grammar, and divergent thoughts.

Capture Immediate Thoughts:

As mentioned previously, this exercise works more powerfully if, rather than writing out the answers to each sentence yourself, you record yourself answering using an audio recorder (many phone apps allow for this) or asking a confidante to read each sentence aloud to you one line at a time. Your confidante or recording would then capture your immediate responses to each line so that they might be written precisely as they were first stated. Responses are to be kept brief, 1-3 sentences to start. You may return and elaborate after completing your first draft of the letter if more details would be helpful or enriching.

The *Release With Love Letter* exercise is best done with your eyes closed so you are less distracted by surrounding stimuli. Your writing partner will write your responses verbatim, so speak slowly and clearly. If your responses get long or difficult for your scribe to record, your partner is to remind you gently to speak slowly and to keep your responses brief. If you don't have a writing partner, no problem. Play back your recording once all components of your letter have been addressed. Write down your answers verbatim before making any changes.

Avoid getting lost in providing background or justifying your writing. No one needs to understand the history or background but you. The more automatic your responses, the more genuine your underlying feelings and needs, and the greater the potential for healing. Many are surprised to realize how beautifully their sentences flow once the letter is complete. Trust the process.

How Much Time to Set Aside:

Once familiar with the *Release With Love Letter* template, writing a complete letter can take under ten minutes, especially when keeping your initial responses *'brief, specific, and to the point.'* Avoid the temptation to spend too much time thinking as your letter is to reflect your automatic thoughts.

Go In Order:

Remember that this exercise deviates from conventional journaling, as it is crafted to capture your most immediate associations to specific prompts around memories of what or who is lost. You are not to write freely but rather to respond with 1-3 sentences initially to each line of the

Release With Love Letter template in order, as outlined (see Appendix for *Release With Love Letter* template with and without added prompts that may be helpful as you learn the process).

Once you have responded to each line of the *Release With Love Letter* in order, you are to consider if any important details about the connection were missed. You may include these and elaborate on them once your letter is complete. You'll notice letters of greatly varying lengths in the examples that follow.

Most importantly, please ensure that your responses are specific. If when asked what you miss or when you think of a loss, you replied in general terms, such as "everything" or "all the time," return and be more specific. Name people, places, or things that call up memories of your loss. Provide your writing partner with a vision of what is most meaningful and vivid in your memory. By the end of the letter, if you remember regrets, wishes, or commitments you *missed* (pun intended), add them.

Complete Each Statement:

It is critical that you complete each line of the template, no matter how difficult. Skipping lines, vague responses, or "I don't know" will interfere with the quality and impact of your letter and may be indicative of the resistance I defined above. Resistance is a barrier to healing. Remember, what we don't look at, we can't heal. You are the only person who can know of the impact of a loss, so push yourself to acknowledge and write down your first thoughts, even if they are hard to admit.

People sometimes get stumped at the 'I wish' or 'I regret' sections. Components can feel especially challenging if you feel anger toward the person or circumstance your letter addresses. Your anger might be in someone having left your life or if you think someone caused you harm. If you feel stuck, I gently remind you that anger may be evidence of unresolved grief. Our work shifts focus away from blame or criticism to personal reflections and healing. Recognize the power you give away over your peace of mind by carrying forth this anger.

As you recognize signs of underlying anger, consider the famous quote attributed to Buddha, *"Anger is like swallowing poison and expecting the other person to die."*[2] A person may have hurt you before. As you continue to focus on that anger or nurture resentment, you allow them to exert influence over your present and future. Let's affirm a different path. When you feel tempted to respond with anger-driven *"you"* responses of blame, attack, or shame, I encourage you instead to incorporate *"I"* statements, like *"I wish that I had…"; "I regret that I did not…";* or simply, *"I wish our life together had felt easier and less painful."*

Your initial reactions to using "I" statements may provoke anger, *"but I'm the one who suffered,"* or *"I didn't do anything, they did"* type of responses. It is in your best interest and highest good to avoid using *"you"* attached to blame and criticism as you write your letter. If you find yourself feeling agitated or focused on wrongs, pause. Take a few deep breaths, and redirect your attention to what you wish you would have done differently or how you wish a situation would have turned out differently. Avoid name-calling or use of the *Release With Love Letter* to blame, shame, or attack a person's memory.

I'll offer one additional perspective here. I believe people are generally good. I also believe that life circumstances, trauma, and wounds may tragically change the course of someone's life and how they show up in relationships with others. When childhood or life has felt unsafe for whatever reason, it is not unusual to develop protective and often

---

[2] The quote "Anger is like swallowing poison and expecting the other person to die" is often attributed to Buddha, but there isn't strong evidence to support that it can be traced back to his teachings. While widely circulated and associated with Buddhist philosophy, its exact origin is uncertain.

distancing strategies to keep others and what is perceived as an unsafe world out. Sometimes what appears to be a mean person is actually a scared, hurt person who doesn't know where or how to feel safe. There is great truth in the quote, *"hurt people hurt people."*[3] I believe those 'hurt' people that go around hurting other people are generally *unhealed* people.

I commend YOU for reading this book, as you are among those motivated to heal. As you work on *your* healing, may you remember the Rumi quote, *"The wound is the place where the light enters you."* May you breathe in that light and connect from that place with all who are around you.

Be Specific:

Be as specific as possible with each line of the *Release with Love Letter*, especially memories and *commitments*. Avoid generalizations like, *"I miss everything."* Instead, recall specific moments and memories, such as a favorite flower, food, color, animal, or shared experience. Recall details like sunsets or how someone's eyes would twinkle when looking at you. The template is designed to crystallize even small moments of comfort or love.

Seldom is anything or anyone all bad. Be diligent in identifying any moments of goodness and connection. Think of memories of missed or unfulfilled longings. You might even wish someone who hurt you had had a better upbringing or childhood so that they had been better prepared to love you in a healthy way.

---

3 The quote "Hurt people hurt people" is often attributed to Dr. Sandra Bloom, a psychiatrist known for her work in trauma-informed care. However, the exact origin of the quote is difficult to trace. It may have been used by various individuals in the field of psychology and mental health. It encapsulates the idea that individuals who have experienced pain or trauma in their own lives may unintentionally perpetuate harm onto others as a result of their unresolved emotional wounds.

"In Your Honor..." – Honor Legacies through Commitments:

I refer to the "*I will honor you and your memory*" section of the letter as the **commitments** section of your letter. I might argue this section is the most important of all. It is the one that captures your intention to honor every moment and every experience moving forward as meaningful. This is where you get to connect your pain to your purpose.

Consider how your experience may shape you moving forward. What are you inspired to be more or less of? Perhaps you'd like to be less like someone who hurt you by being more respectful, loving, and emotionally present to those around you. Perhaps you want to be more generous, expressive, active, or adventurous like someone lost. Perhaps you'll commit to honoring self-care and mental health to honor someone who missed opportunities to prioritize this.

The *commitments* section of each *Release With Love Letter* is the section that calls you to decide how you will allow the effects of your loss to define your life. It is where you affirm that your loss will not be in vain. When completing the *commitments* section, referring to what you wrote in the wishes and regrets section is helpful and meaningful in connecting your pain to purpose.

Your wishes and regrets often inform what you commit to affirming. If you regret not saying 'I love you' more, commit to telling loved ones regularly today and in the future that you love them. If you wish you would have called or spent more time with whoever is gone, commit to spending more quality, uninterrupted time with people in your life today. The idea is to move toward living with less predictable regrets.

Commitments are most impactful if you identify observable, measurable ways to incorporate them into your life daily or weekly. This means you are not simply identifying thoughts but words and actions. You might start each day in honor of loved ones who passed away by voicing a gratitude statement, a prayer, a joke, or playing music motivated by their memory. Clients have shared that they dance to their late partner's favorite song while baking. Others talk to hummingbirds and butterflies in their yards as a comforting means of connection. I've had others commit to going to a comedy show or sentimental location on anniversary dates of reminders of meaningful moments. The location was determined by specific memories related in the first section of the letter.

Suppose you are grieving someone who caused harm. In that case, your commitment might be to explicitly express compassion and empathy towards others in unique ways every day. You might look to positively impact someone's life daily or weekly by volunteering or writing letters to seniors. You might pursue advocacy work or tend to a garden.

As you work to heal your wounds especially on the more challenging days, consider one of my favorite nuggets of wisdom attributed to Cynthia Occelli[4]:

> *"For a seed to achieve its greatest expression, it must come completely undone. The shell cracks, its insides come out and everything changes. To someone who doesn't understand growth, it would look like complete destruction."*

Each person's journey toward healing and connection to purpose will be different and symbolic. What will you make yours mean?

Have Your Letter Read Back To You:

Once all core aspects are written, have your letter read back to you either by your confidante or via recording, if possible. See how it feels to hear it, with your eyes closed. Feel free to add or edit wording however you see fit once the letter is written so the letter flows grammatically and feels

---

4 While often attributed to Cynthia Occelli, there is a lack of clarity around a specific citation in her works. This quote may have been paraphrased or summarized from her writings or speeches.

impactful. Be prepared, many clients tear up when they hear their letter read back to them. This is good; no, this is great. This is healing. Allow it. Embrace it.

If you are satisfied with your letter, it may help to record yourself reading the letter aloud so you can listen to the recording in the days/weeks to follow. A phone audio recorder app or other electronic device is most helpful.

In the majority of instances, you will not be sending your letter to the person to whom it's addressed. These letters are intended solely for your healing journey and can be securely stored or safely and ceremoniously destroyed. I've had clients who chose to share their letters at funerals, bringing comfort and gratitude to grieving family members through the sentiments expressed.

In rare cases, you may share your letter with the person to whom it was addressed. Exercise caution if you choose to do so. Ensure that it's crafted with love, carries a positive tone, focuses on sentimental commitments, and is likely to be well-received. If there is any hint of judgment, criticism, or statements of "I wish you would have" or "I'll think of you as a reminder of what not to do," I strongly advise against sharing the letter with that person. This could be retraumatizing and add to your pain. What feels tender and heartfelt to you might be perceived differently by another. It's best to keep your words sacred in these moments.

What If It's Not Yet Lost?

What I find especially intriguing about the power of this intervention is that you need not wait until a loss has occurred to write a *Release With Love Letter*. Writing a letter can encourage you to be proactively mindful and intentional about what you want to honor in an existing relationship. You may imagine what you would miss or regret if the tie were gone. Use this wisdom to guide future choices and **commit** to doing better.

Consider changes you'd be willing to make to avoid taking essential aspects of your relationship for granted. End the commitment sections of these adapted letters by stating, *"…and I will start today."*

After Writing…

Read your *Release With Love Letter* daily for at least 1-2 weeks, then periodically from there. It can help to email yourself the letter and to keep it in your inbox or as a text on your phone as a reminder to keep reading it. Pay particular attention to *commitments*. Affirm these daily to inspire healing.

Continue to practice reading and internalizing the *commitments* section of your letter as a guide for changes you will intentionally make as you heal and develop your best self. Each time you read and honor your *commitments*, you will affirm that your pain, memories, and experiences will not have been wasted. Your grief will be purposed for your higher good and that of those touched by you in your healing.

Whether you choose to share your letter with a trusted confidante or opt to save or destroy it, remain mindful of honoring your *commitments* as you work towards acceptance and closure. Whatever you decide, remember to *Release With Love.*

Recognize Calls and Expressions of Love:

Before we move on to the letters, I'd like to share one final nugget of wisdom. Drawn from A Course in Miracles, published in the 1970s, consider every action as either an expression of love or a call for love. Calls for love can be misunderstood and can contribute to pain and loss in relationships when not expressed in clear, vulnerable, or healthy ways.

Consideration of calls for love and acts of love may inform your *commitments*. You might, for example, honor a person's memory by choosing to show more acts of love as were expressed to you. As for calls for love, you might consider that someone's hurtful patterns or possible outbursts may have been misguided efforts to feel safe, that is, to get you to *see* them, love them, or comfort them. As such, in the "I wish" section, you might consider: "I wish we had learned how to communicate in gentle, loving ways. I wonder if we might still be together," or "I wish we hadn't fought so much. I know you were in pain. I wish I could have heard what you felt or needed in a way that brought us closer. I wish I would have asked more questions about how you were doing," or "I wish we had gone to therapy. I wanted so much for us to stay in each other's lives."

Notice how lamenting what was or wasn't without villainizing or victimization connects you more to your empathic heart space. The goal is to recognize what you wished for while identifying the other person's likely misdirected efforts to feel safe or meet their own underlying needs.

Grief is a natural response and often proportional to love lost. I embrace the pain I feel in my father's absence. What would it say about his legacy if it were easy to lose him? I welcome pain and grief as reminders that I had the best father I could have asked for.

Cliff notes:

As you prepare to get started, notice how you feel inside. Feel the weight of your emotions. As you begin writing, focus your letter one line at a time to identify each element of your grief. Respond with only a few words at a time. Move from one line to the next. Don't stop to think about your responses. Go with the first thoughts that come to mind, and trust that they will come together when your letter is complete.

If possible, have someone read your completed letter back to you or listen to a recording of yourself reading it. Afterward, ask yourself if the weight of your emotions feels even 1% lighter. If not, I suggest you expand on the *commitments* section and connect your commitments to your regrets and longings. The idea is to move forward with fewer regrets in future relationships. Read your letter in the days and weeks that follow and work toward honoring any commitments you set as you become the healthiest version of yourself.

As you go to the next page with the *Release With Love Letter* template, consider playing soft or classical music. This can aid in concentration and emotional connection as you begin your letter. I wish you courage and focus as you proceed.

RELEASE WITH LOVE LETTER

The *Release With Love Letter* template below is reprinted in the Appendix with and without prompts to aid in your completion of the writing.

Dear *[name the person you are grieving]*,

What I miss about you most is …
What I regret most is …
I wish …
I remember you each time I …

[It can help keep you present in the moment if you restate name here],
You made me a better person by …

I will honor you and your memory by …
[I refer to this as the **commitments** *section wherein you identify how you will consider purposeful change in memory of that which is lost. It can help to refer back to the regrets and wish sections above to complete this. This connects your pain to purpose.]*

Thank you for being my …
[identify who the person you are grieving is to you.]

I release you with love and pray for your peace …
[until we meet again…this last part can be eliminated or modified based on your belief system.]

Love,
[Your name as the person you are grieving would have known you]

Ok, are you ready to bear witness to the reflective and healing experience of *Releasing with Love?*

Chapter 3:
What do 'Release With Love' letters look like?

In the following pages, you'll find samples of various *Release With Love Letters* written by clients and loved ones. Each person provided me consent to include their writing for your review. Each letter has been reproduced in its authentic form, with names redacted to protect privacy—no letters are fabricated for entertainment purposes.

I was nearly moved to tears and inspired by my clients' reactions when asked for permission to include their letters in this book. Below is one of my favorite responses from a client:

"Oh gosh, I would love that! That made my day. This made me think it's not just about me. Wow. I've been depressed for so long! I would love to know my work can help others."

You might be wondering, why would I want or need to read others' letters? Well, you certainly don't have to, but when doing this exercise on your own, it can be difficult to stay positively-focused and goal-directed. Seeing examples of letters that were directed through the process can be helpful. I also thought you'd appreciate hearing from others on their experience of the writing process.

TESTIMONIALS

Below is a touching response to inviting friends to write their own *Release With Love Letters* without my oversight. Spoiler alert: her letter to her daughter in the following pages may evoke an emotional response.

"Writing it was definitely challenging but good. I resisted the feelings pretty significantly. It's easier to pretend that my pain, fear, and disappointment isn't there. Confronting it takes courage and forces denial to flee. I don't want to cry about it anymore.... but pretending I'm ok isn't a great answer either. Intellectually, I knew who my letter needed to be to. Emotionally, I didn't want to confront it.

As I wrote, I was ok at the start. Then, I started to feel sad and overwhelmed and wanted to rush through it in order to avoid negative feelings. In doing so, I missed steps and had to go back. Going back helped me to slow back down and be ok with laying down the intensity of feelings. And reading it today is definitely less intense."

Incidentally, when asked how reading others' letters may have helped her in writing her own, this friend shared:

"Reading the letters of others really helped me to not feel alone in my grief. Seeing how others have processed helped me to better formulate my own thoughts and feelings as I began my letter and healing journey."

Another friend who wrote a letter to her late mother found the *Release With Love Letter* helpful in identifying unresolved guilt. In having followed the prompts outlined in the template, she found:

"I literally just started spewing words. It was interesting. It all flowed pretty naturally. I wondered if I should have proofread it more or analyzed it, but then I wanted it in its raw form…I probably could write 500 pages of what reminds me of her…I just let the words flow out of my mind onto the page using the prompts…

It felt good to write, and it was interesting when I got to the 'I wish' part. I realized I definitely didn't have closure. That was really nice to write on the page…It felt really good to write. I'm in a really good place."

This writer connected in the *commitments* section with intentional ways of honoring her mother's legacy. She illuminates how vital it is to resist critique or review while writing the letter's first draft. Doing so would have distracted her from capturing raw emotions by redirecting her focus to proofreading or thinking too deeply into responses. I encourage you to record your immediate, automatic responses one line at a time until the template is complete.

Remember that you have the opportunity to adapt or add to your letter *after* it is written in its entirety and read back. Completing the letter before elaborating or making changes is more likely to highlight the essence of your feelings.

RECEIVE WITH LOVE FOLLOW-UP

A powerful follow-up to the *Release With Love Letter* exercise is to draft an 'imagined' response. This would be a response from the person you addressed your letter to. There is a catch; this may not be a realistic response.

I would like you to imagine the healthiest version of that person responding. What would their most evolved self say? Beyond defenses, fears, and underlying tendencies toward hurt or anger, what might their tender, possibly even scared inner child say? What might that person have wanted or needed that may have been poorly expressed from a place of woundedness?

The follow-up letter, referred to as the *Receive with Love Letter,* embodies how the recipient of your *Release With Love Letter* might respond. There is no template for this, though it may help to respond to your *Release With Love Letter* one line or section at a time.

Close your eyes as you ponder the response. Again, consider lighting a candle or playing soft music in the background as you imagine what words you might hear back. You are to tap into the most sensitive, tender essence of the person or dream that is lost.

We often fear the worst-case scenario and forget any signs of goodness when we are afraid, angry, or resentful. You may be shocked to realize what flows out of you if you seek the innocent humanness present in moments, even if only in childhood before wounds were imposed.

I hope you find hope, comfort, and direction in the *Receive with Love Letter* examples that follow.

On to the Letters...

RECEIVE WITH LOVE LETTERS

I leave you here with love and light as you embrace the intimate truths shared by those who have entrusted me before you. Where additional testimonials about the writing experience are available, I have included them in Italics along with their respective writings below. May you experience catharsis and appreciate the emotional journey that lies ahead.

Dear Estranged Daughter,

What I miss about you most is the way you light up a room when you are doing well. Your joy is contagious, and you think of others so readily. You are eager to connect and do things with me and your siblings. What I regret most is not knowing how to handle your behaviors and mental illness in ways that honored my boundaries but allowed you to feel loved and heard.

I wish we could understand one another and put our love before our differences. I wish you would come around for holidays and that you would allow your daughter to receive the love I have to give her. I remember you each time I see a toy monkey. I remember you when I think back to our old houses or to when your siblings were small and looked up to you so much. I remember you each time I drive by the last house you lived in just a few miles away.

Daughter, you made me a better person by teaching me that somethings are too big and painful to simply overcome. You taught me that love isn't enough in a relationship, but that skills, understanding and a lot of work are needed in complicated relationships. You taught me that I needed to learn more in order to show up differently for your siblings than I did for you at times. I will honor you by continuing to make myself available to you if you choose. I honor you by freeing myself of the grief and hurt between us so that I am fully available for your siblings whom you love.

Thank you for being me daughter. I prayed to receive you and adopt you. You are a blessing and a gift and always have been. I release you with love and pray for your peace and our healthy reconnection while we still have a chance. I release you with love and peace even if you choose not to reconnect on this side of heaven.

Dear Dad,

What I miss most about you is our car rides to the gym…being able to talk to you about all the stuff, being a boss, a dad, and a husband. I miss seeing you with the kids. I miss having you at our son's games. I miss seeing you with Mom and the girls. I miss having you on our family vacations. I miss being home and seeing, well hearing, you come in the garage door with a Polar Pop. I miss having you to talk to after another gut-wrenching ND loss or disappointing Cardinal's season.

What I regret most is that you don't get to see our son grow up and play sports. I regret that you don't get to throw him batting practice or teach him baseball. You would have had so much fun watching him play, it really is a joy. You would be so proud of him. I regret that you didn't get to meet my youngest and you never got to see my daughters grow up, that you don't get to be goofy with them and have inside jokes with them. You would laugh and laugh and laugh with them and the girls with you, it would be a blast. I regret not being able to talk to you about the challenges of being a dad and a husband. You would have had great perspective. I regret that you did not see me continue my career arc or where I am today. I regret that you didn't get to see the girls become moms or meet their darling little girls. I regret that I never get to see you and mom celebrate retirement together. I miss your stories. You were a great storyteller.

I wish you would have gotten the help that you asked for. I wish you would have made it just another day or another week. I think you would have been okay. I wish you were here today. I wish you were here for the ups and downs to help support and love us and to continue to make a difference. I wish you were here for Mom for all the challenges the last 5 years have held.

I remember you each time I take our son to batting practice. I remember you each time I have something to fix in the sink. I remember you each time the needle drops on the record player. I remember you each time I hear "Heard it through the Grapevine" or "Sympathy for the Devil" or really any Bee Gees song, you loved music. I remember you each time I see someone (successfully) raising a flag up a flagpole. I remember you every St. Patrick's Day, how much you loved that holiday and seemingly all things Irish. You made me a better person by teaching me the value of hard work, by getting up with me at 5am every day to do the paper route. You taught me the importance of education by going back and sacrificing while you had a family and were getting master's degrees. You taught me the importance of exercise, of exercising with your family, especially your wife. You taught me how important spending time with your wife is, especially in the little moments. You taught me to dress for success. You taught me it's ok to have a slice, just so long as you know how to play it and angle it over the house to drop it right in the fairway.

Dad, I will honor you and your memory by continuing to be the best husband, dad, and leader I can be, by raising my family in faith. I will honor you by prioritizing my physical and mental health, throughout my life, to always be there for the ones I love. I will honor you by reaching out, checking in, making sure people really are ok. I will honor you by trying to make people feel special no matter their title, every person I cross. I will honor you by loving my family, Mom, the girls. I will honor you by pursuing excellence in all that I do.

Thank you for being my dad. Thank you for always setting an example for those around you, for teaching us you can make a difference, 1 person at a time.

I release you with love and pray for your peace until we meet again.

After writing, this client expressed gratitude for the opportunity to complete a Release With Love Letter, "It was a fun and emotional experience."

Dearest reader, if you or someone you know is experiencing thoughts of suicide or recurring thoughts of death, please seek immediate help from a qualified mental health professional, proceed to your nearest emergency room, or contact a suicide prevention hotline such as the 988 Suicide & Crisis Lifeline. The 988 dialing code, designated by Congress in 2020, connects those experiencing distress or crisis to free, confidential 24-7 support through the National Suicide Prevention Lifeline. Call or text 988 or chat 988lifeline.org to speak to someone in your time of need and be reminded that there is hope. Help is available, you are wanted, and you are not alone. Please find this resource among others in Appendix D: Grief Management Resources.

The act of suicide has far-reaching implications for those who love you and generations to follow. Many peoples' lives, including those you haven't yet met, will be profoundly affected by your absence. Please consider the weight and beauty of this sentiment. You were created because you are needed, even if you don't know how or why yet. Remember that every emotion comes in waves. Tomorrow is a new day. Just for today, allow yourself to feel your emotions without judgment.

Dear Brother,

What I miss most about you is your sense of humor and your ability to stir the pot without pissing everybody off.

What I regret most is that we didn't have more time. Before you got sick, I assumed we had all the time in the world. I regret not going out of my way to make time for you.

I wish you could be here to give me shit about a container home. I wish you were here to drive my Tesla around and see how much fun it is. I wish you could have met my boyfriend. I wish we had more time.

I remember you each time I see a Kansas City Royales baseball game. I think of you each time I hear our nephews talk about money. I remember you each time we go to the lake for a family vacation. I think of you each time there's a big milestone. You just pop up to startle me, like when you turn on the TV. Thank you for not doing that anymore.

You made me a better person by showing me how to love a partner; by holding me accountable but letting me be myself.

I will honor you and your memory by continuing to talk about you and laugh about some of the crazy shit you've done. I will honor you by taking the kids on their 17th birthday trip even if it's late, by keeping my promise to stay in touch with your wife and make sure she knows that she is still loved.

I will take the time to go home for 2-3 weeks at a time to spend time with family. In your honor I will tell people I love them more often whether by text or call. I won't wait for a reason to reach out. Each time my dog and I go for a ride I'll picture you back there with him.

Thank you for being my brother and friend. I release you with love and pray for your peace until we meet again.

Dear Ex-Boyfriend,

What I miss about you most is how it felt laying in your arms and how you'd hold my hand whenever we were in the car together. I loved how cuddly we were. I loved the safety of your touch and your sacrificial heart. I miss how close to me you felt when we read together and when we shared our fears…when we both felt safe in moments.

What I regret is not expressing myself and my fears in a way that you could hear me. I regret not carrying myself better when I was frustrated. I was so scared you'd leave. I just kept pushing you away, thinking it would hurt less that way, but it didn't.

I wish we had both tried harder. I wish we had practiced how to communicate better the right way. Sometimes, it just felt like we went through the motions, but our pride kept us from being present and supportive in the ways we each needed. I wish we could have truly seen and heard one another in the ways our hearts yearned to be seen. I wish we had created more safety in our relationship. I wish I felt like you knew my heart. I wish I had protected your inner child and mine. We could have been great together. Everything was just so hard.

I think of you each time I go to a comedy show, pass a sushi restaurant, or see a teddy bear. You tried so hard to make me happy. It's sad that I didn't feel seen by you, but I know you tried…you tried so hard, and I'll never forget that. Your intentions were pure. You made me a better person by modeling self-sacrifice for people we love. You always tried to show up with a nonverbal cue of your dedication to me…roses, a snack, wearing an outfit you thought I'd like…some peace offering letting me know how desperately you wanted us to repair and heal from our hurts. That was never lost on me. A rose was never just a rose. It was you letting me know you weren't done and that you were still there for me and for us. I will forever thank you for that. You were so strong for us.

I will honor the time we shared by forever working on being a better communicator and creating safety in my relationships. I will express myself and affirm my partners in ways that help them feel accepted for their authentic selves. I will suspend my urge to react when hurt and will remain open to compromise around my partners' needs. I will share my feelings lovingly and in a dignified way, especially when I feel unhappy. I will work on asking for what I want in gentle ways.

Moving forward, I will be courageous in speaking my truth and detaching with love, when appropriate. I will express myself lovingly when concerned about compatibility. I will focus on connecting, not correcting. I will help my partner be my hero. I will strive to see beauty in moments, especially when it is hardest to see. I will breathe in that beauty, cherish more of what is, and welcome more surprises. I commit to showing up with love and ensuring that the lessons learned in our relationship are not wasted. I will forever miss and love you.

Thank you for sharing our soul connection. I release you with love and pray for your peace as we navigate the complex and rich journey of life and love.

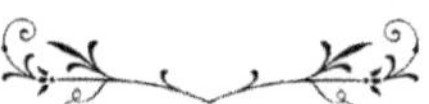

Dear Son,

What I miss most about you is everything. I miss the time we shared. I loved helping you. I miss working with you. I was so grateful that you let me help you with your business. Your work was your everything, and I loved being a part of that.

What I regret most is not knowing what happened to you. Everything happened so suddenly. It was a shock for me. For everybody. I wish you were still here with me.

I remember you each time I see things in the house you would have done for me. You fixed anything that broke down. You loved helping me. I don't have anyone to help me now. You were always there for me. We were always together.

You made me a better person by loving me as your mother. You inspired me to be more helpful to those less fortunate. You did so much for others. You did so much good for the world.

I will honor you by noticing the goodness around me every day. Whenever anyone does help me with anything that I need, I will consider that perhaps they are an angel sent by you. I will keep your legacy alive and pray that your soul uplifts daily.

Thank you for being my son. I'm so proud of you.

I release you with love and pray for your peace until we meet again.

Dear Mommy,

What I miss about you most is your unconditional love, support, and guidance.

What I regret most is our last day together. Never did I think it would be our last and we left on terms that never have given me closure. I needed one last talk to discuss everything from your visit.

I wish I could go back to that day and give you a huge hug and thank you for everything you had set up for me that weekend. I wish we could have had the holiday we were planning just a few weeks later. I wish it was a better ending if it was going to be my last day with you.

I remember you each time I do pretty much anything! You are all around me in so many things I do in life, I see in life, and discover in life! I could think of 1000 things that remind me of you, but sunflowers especially! You always called me your 'sunflower' and got me sunflowers, and I always thought of you as my 'sunflower.' The meaning behind it was that you were like the flower that lit up the day and brightened up our lives…just a happy flower that seems to breathe life and last forever. Today sunflowers make me so happy. It's like the "You are my sunshine" song. Every time I see a sunflower I get them in your honor, and now my husband gifts them to me as a loving reminder of your presence.

Mommy, you made me a better person by showing me true genuine acceptance of others. You showed me how to love deeply and to always find the positives through the darkness. Mommy, I will honor you and your memory by always telling stories about you and celebrating your birthday and the day you became my guardian angel. I will honor you by spreading the love and joy you loved sharing with people. I will cherish each moment with the special people in my life and not take things for granted. I will not worry about the small things. I know there are so many beautiful blessings surrounding me. I will always strive to be a more caring, understanding, deeper person, like you lived your life.

Thank you for being my Mommy and best friend. I release you with love and keep you in my heart forever.

This friend described the process of writing: "Reading the questions and writing, I was surprised by how nicely everything flowed from my brain to my pencil. The regret part was interesting. That flowed really organically as well. I almost worried that it was too easy, that I wasn't doing it right, and that I may need to go back and overanalyze, but I didn't. It felt really nice to write that."

Dear Doggie,

What I miss most about you is your smile. You had such a funny little smile. Your teeth were like human teeth.

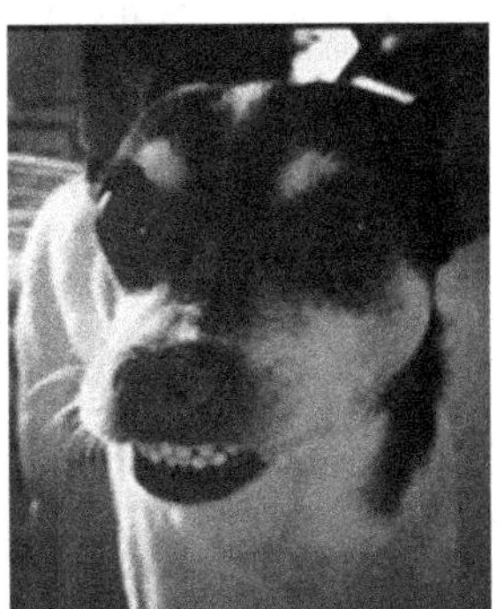

What I regret most is how I lost you. I will always wonder if I lost you too soon. As a Vet, I'll always wonder if there was more I could have done and if I gave you the best care possible. Even though no one saw what happened to you, I wonder if I could have managed things differently for a different outcome.

I wish I could hold you again.

I remember you each time I see another rat terrier or whenever I see hummingbirds in my parents' backyard.

You made me a better person by giving me your love. You accepted me right away when I picked you up at that hotel. It's like you hopped into the car and simply and lovingly accepted your new life with me.

I think about you when I support my clients in their grief over the sudden loss of their pets. You helped me understand how to be with and relate to that kind of pain. My sister and I bought a bench and a plaque in your honor. It was meant for outside, but it actually sits in my parents living room. We always keep your memory close.

I will honor you and your memory by seeing you in each of my clients and doing my best to give them love and help them feel safe in their times of medical need.

Thank you for being my friend. Thank you for always letting me know you're with me. I'll never look at a bird the same. I release you with love and pray for your peace until we meet again.

Dear Pre-Hysterectomy Self,

What I want most is for you to know how much I appreciate you and how far you've brought me. What I regret most is not listening to my body sooner. I can't help but wonder if the outcome would be the same if I would have listened sooner. Maybe if I had taken responsibility for my feelings sooner, this wouldn't be so hard. I wish to heal from this. I wish for days without cramps, anemia, and discomfort. I look forward to physical health. I will remember you each time I look at my babies.

You have made me a better person by keeping me grounded. You have made me a better person by pushing me to reach out for support. You're keeping me humble.

I will honor you by taking the 5 minutes a day to feel and to lovingly parent my inner child. I will welcome all of my feelings tenderly and accept them all. I will model healthy grief and adaptability that I would like my children to see. I want them to see me vulnerable and healthy.

Thank you for being my friend and partner in life. I release you with love and pray for your peace as we go through this journey of life together.

This friend invited me to walk her through a Release With Love Letter as she expressed shame for her feelings and sadness around accepting the need for a partial hysterectomy. After writing her letter, she expressed surprise about the feelings that surfaced. Tearfully, she voiced: "Wow, I didn't expect the guilt!" She hadn't realized how heavily she was shaming her inner child for needing to grieve or the meaning she had given this procedure. She shared disappointment with her reaction: "the shame's coming out right now."

Only moments after having her letter read back to her, this friend breathed with greater relief: "I feel so much lighter!" Allowing herself permission to feel was so critical to acceptance and moving forward. She recognized that her shame lifted as she was able to name it. She connected with a motivation to heal: "I need to talk to my inner child and let her feelings matter. I need to let her cry."

My friend wrote me the next day: "I felt goosebumps reading this again. I'm feeling like a weight has been lifted off of me. I'm still melancholy but feel better about allowing myself to just feel melancholy and be ok. Thank you for helping me feel safe to speak about this."

One week later, this same friend shared that she went to her doctor to discuss her final decision. She said the doctor helped her feel "comfortable with the decision from a medical standpoint. So, overall, with my daily reading [of the Release With Love Letter], I'm getting less and less triggered by the thought of letting my uterus go."

Only moments before I uploaded the final manuscript for publication, this friend again blessed me with further feedback as she expressed her deep appreciation for my introducing her to the Release With Love Letter process: "You'd never believe this—I had a breakthrough! I've been reading my letter morning and night, and today at lunch, I didn't start crying when my girlfriend asked how I was doing about my impending situation. I actually felt really positive when discussing my decision to go through with it. I started crying because I'm _not_ feeling the shame/guilt like I was!! … I can see the difference now reading the letter…I understand why you have me doing that now." What a testament to the importance of continuing to read and honor your statement in the days and weeks following your writing.

Dear Father,

What I miss about you most is the ease with which you went through life. You never seemed to hold onto grudges. You were generally kind to people. Everyone always told me how much you loved me. They would tell me I was your favorite.

What I regret most is that I never felt comfortable or safe around you. I regret that many of my memories of you involve criticism and pain.

I wish I had felt at ease around you. I wish I had memories of deep conversations with you. I am grateful my daughter had this with her father. I wish I could have talked to you the way she talked with her dad. There always seemed to be so much distance between us.

I remember you each time I feel insecure. Sometimes I dream about you. Those dreams are usually unpleasant. There is a sense of coldness. I'll usually wake up with a lingering sadness and sense of relief that I'm awake.

You made me a better person by teaching me what I wanted in a husband and in a father for my child. I'm happy that I was able to marry a man who was your opposite. My husband was everything for my daughter that I wanted from you. None of the differences with my husband mattered because he was such a good man and father. He was everything you were not. It's confusing because you were overall a good father. You never wanted to leave our mother or abandon our family, and you provided anything we wanted. I just wish I felt safer around you.

I will honor you and your memory by forgiving you. I don't think you meant to leave me feeling uncomfortable. I pray that you have peace wherever you are. In your memory, I will strive to create a safer environment where my daughter can come to me with her feelings. I will honor you by enjoying conversations and making memories with her.

Thank you for being my father. I release you with love and pray for your peace until we meet again.

I feel especially honored to have had my mother write a letter to my father for the book. I did my best to honor her sentiments as I translated her letter below from Farsi to English. After writing, my mother shared:

"It was really interesting. I wasn't quite sure what to say. It brought to life many of the memories I hold about your father. I got a bit emotional as I got choked up. That caught me off guard. I think of him and those memories often, but I never cry over them. It just always seemed like I was reminiscing, but it was interesting that I cried. It was a nice release. I feel lighter." And my mother wrote…

Dearest Husband Joon,

What I miss about you most is your jokes and sense of humor. You were so playful. I miss how you'd tell me you loved me so much. You would joke that your love for me was so deep, you would eat poison out of my hands. You understood my dark sense of humor in a way that no one else ever has. I miss how important I felt to you. You often said that it was because of me that you made it to 85 years old. I miss how you always had my back. You saw the best in me always. Even when I offered to change for you, you joked that you'd never want that as you accepted my every quality as simply a part of who I am.

What I regret most is not hugging and kissing you more. I wish I knew the depths of my love for you when you were alive. I wish I told you I loved you more. I regret the day you woke up blind in one eye. Those last few years were so hard. I can't drive by a hospital or the rehab center without thinking of you. I felt so helpless when you were there. There is so much more I wish I could have done for you.

I had promised you we'd never place you outside of our home in your later years. I wish the doctors didn't force us to move you. That was heart-wrenching. I felt like I'd broken my promise to you. I'm so grateful that later when I brought you home to visit with me, you asked to return to the group home after we enjoyed our meal. You were so relaxed and comfortable. It was clear you'd forgotten by then where home was. You gave me such a gift by letting me know you were at ease where you were.

I remember you each time I look at sugar cubes, tea, and roses. I always think of you when I see a toothpick. From the time I knew you, you always seemed to have a toothpick between your teeth so you could keep them clean. At first, I thought you were ridiculous. Now, I wish so much that I could see that again. I remember you each time something breaks down around the house. I am reminded that you are not here to fix it. I wish you were here. You made life simpler. I wish you were here for when I have hard days or when I feel misunderstood. You were my confidante and best friend. I could trust you with anything. I wish I had you to talk to. You were always so kind and able to give me new perspectives and patience in a way that I felt supported and accepted by you always. You were never easily swayed and were so good at keeping the peace.

You made me a better person by never trying to change me. You accepted me for all my good and bad. I miss how you'd joke that the scorpion couldn't help but sting…that to sting was its pure nature. Even when I offered to change for you, you asked me not to. You insisted you always wanted me just as I came.

I will honor you by always keeping your memory alive. I will keep talking about you to my friends in ways that capture who you were to me. I will prepare your favorite dishes when I entertain guests. I will honor you by striving to create memories in the years to come with our daughter as we keep your passions and hobbies alive.

Thank you for being my husband and best friend in life. I release you with love and pray for your peace until we meet again.

I felt so moved by my mother's letter that I researched the proverb to which she refers above. I found its roots in the Persian fable 'The Scorpion and the Turtle,' drawn from a collection of fables called Anvaar Soheilithat, written around 1500. The Persian proverb suggests that a scorpion's nature is to sting. It does what it was created to do.

I so enjoyed reading the Wikipedia synopsis of this proverb after reading my mother's letter that I thought I would share it with you:

A scorpion wants to cross a river but cannot swim, so it asks a frog to carry it across. The frog hesitates, afraid that the scorpion might sting it, but the scorpion promises not to, pointing out that it would drown if it killed the frog in the middle of the river. The frog considers this argument sensible and agrees to transport the scorpion.

Midway across the river, the scorpion stings the frog anyway, dooming them both. The dying frog asks the scorpion why it stung despite knowing the consequence, to which the scorpion replies: "I am sorry, but I couldn't resist the urge. It's my character."

What a powerful reminder to see and accept others as they are!

Below, you'll find my letter to my father—my hero—the man who taught me the definition of class, self-respect, empathy, compassion, and to believe in myself. You'll notice my letter is quite lengthy. Once you've written enough of these, it'll be easier to allow creativity to flow while remaining loyal to the template. Do be sure to keep your letter positively focused and affirm purpose-driven commitments.

Dearest Daddy,

What I miss most about you is your playfulness and how you couldn't help but blush when I walked into a room. It was nearly impossible for you not to smile around me. I've never felt another love like that...your love saw beyond pain, sadness, and stress to simply a sense of joy and freedom. The safety I felt with you is unmatched. My love for you was and is so massive.

Daddy, what I regret most is not finding a way to keep you at home. Thinking about the hours you spent alone, confused and possibly scared, in the group home breaks my heart. I regret that mom and I weren't given the time or space together to figure out a different plan of care for you or at least to feel at peace with the decisions doctors made. We felt so strongarmed into such a life-changing and abrupt move. We were terrified and always wanted to do right by you. I regret feeling the rug pulled up from under us at the hospital the day we were told you couldn't return home safely. Maybe the doctors were right, but I don't know if I'll ever feel settled around this, because it was all so sudden.

Daddy, I hate how those last years happened. Every year seemed to come with another scare or deep loss. I wish I could still sit with you, look at you, talk with you about boys, hear your wisdom and how you'd tease me, "Elish, they're not short. You're tall." I loved your daddy-isms. I'll forever find comfort and smile when I think of your famous line anytime I was hurt, sad, or frustrated: "Bozorg Mishi, Yadet Mire" *(Farsi-English translation: "You'll grow up and forget about it.")*. Well, I certainly haven't forgotten you.

I can still hear your sweet voice when you'd tease me. You had the most gentle, loving way of offering unique perspectives, always leading with your endearing, "Well you know MonkeyFace..." lessons. You were always so loving to me and everyone around you. You never saw status and you treated everyone you met with such respect and kindness. I've never met a gentler soul than you. Everyone loved you, but no one knew you like me and mom.

Daddy, you were so quiet, so poised, intimidating to some because you always looked so serious. But to me, you were simply my sweet daddy. I loved being your MonkeyFace…your pearl as you wrote me in that poem when I turned 16. You were always so poetic. Thank you for passing on to me your gift with words and passion for passion.

I remember you each time I challenge myself to be better, to be gentler, to be more patient and accepting. I remember you each time I wish for more kindness in the world and choose to lead by example even when it hurts to do so. I wish there were more people like you. My world feels so unsafe without you in it. I feel like I'll never again experience the same ease and sense of security around feeling loved that I once did with you. I remember you each time I think of (or gobble up) fried chicken skin, each time I see a duck or a swan or when I pass by a lake. I think of you each time I see a shih tzu, a farm animal, or gaze into my dog's eyes. I think of you when I look at tomatoes, drown my salads in lime juice, and enjoy French Onion Soup or Roquefort blue cheese. I think of you and smile when I giggle over my days of taking LSAT practice exams and answering the questions at the front of the encyclopedia for fun. You always found joy in my passion for learning. We shared so many crazy dreams! I cherish how much I am like you.

Daddy, you taught me to delight in so many simple pleasures. I love the memory of how hard you laughed when you realized I'd spent 45 minutes giggling and gabbing away with a random telemarketer and when you'd tease me to stop talking the electrician's ear off because you were paying him by the hour. You joked that I'd wear out my future partner with my chattiness, but you loved it. As much as you loved hearing me talk and how I connected with strangers, I also know you worried that I'd let the wrong people in.

Daddy, it was so obvious how much joy mom and I brought you. I never questioned your adoration. You made me a better person by offering me a guide for who and how I want to be. Every day I strive to be more like the image I have of you. You weren't perfect. You made mistakes. But you were so kind to others and to yourself. You had a heart of gold and always walked with your head held high. You always modeled doing the right thing.

You cared about people no matter their status and treated everyone with respect. You wanted everyone around you to feel appreciated and seen. I remember how excited your staff's children would get when you walked into the office on family days. I remember how jealous I'd get when they'd run to hug your legs. God, you were so special!

What was especially unique about you was that even in your grace, you never let anyone walk over you. You fought for what you deserved and refused to settle for mediocrity. I remember the day you challenged your boss for a less-than outstanding rating that you knew was based on discrimination…and of course, you won! I definitely have your fire in me daddy. You taught me values of excellence, passion, compassion, and diversification. You taught me to be a visionary, a strong writer, an advocate, and an influencer. You taught me to have impact.

Daddy, thank you for the gifts you left behind in your most delicate moments of life. I will never forget the conversations we shared in the emergency room after your fall. You seemed so calm yet must have been so confused. I tried to keep your mind off of where we are. I'll never forget how when I asked, "Daddy, what are your favorite memories in life?" you responded simply, "*You.*"

I remember how you'd always tease that you'd never be ready for Azrael[5] and that you planned to live forever. You extended me such a gift before your surgery that last week. You so calmly and playfully joked with me: "Ok, Elish. Let's go, I'm ready. Let's go." "But daddy, where are you going?" I knew that day what you meant. I felt an eerie calm around your ease. Even in your hardest moments, you were protective of me and mom and let us know in your own ways that we need not worry.

Daddy, I will honor you and your memory by pausing before I speak, honoring silence, listening for what others may have to say before I speak. I will use fewer words, particularly when upset. I will ask questions more than I make statements. I will ask myself daily, "how would daddy respond?" I will seek to show kindness always. I will seek to be gentler in my word, calmer and softer in my tone.

In your honor, I will consider others' feelings, remembering that tomorrow is not promised. I will look for what I may admire in every person that crosses my path. I will work toward writing a letter like this every time I am hurt or upset in hopes that I take no one for granted. I will remind myself to act without regrets regardless of possible outcomes. I will carry myself with integrity so I can feel proud when I lay my head down each night.

Daddy, because of our family's experience, I will be extra diligent and sensitive to my clients' experiences as they age. I will take every opportunity with clients and friends to help ease them and their families through navigating the complex and often life-altering decisions they'll face as they age. I will use the pain mom and I endured around end-of-life planning to guide clients through the difficult, vulnerable moments that are so hard to talk about. I will lead with grace, confidence, understanding, and patience, making sure their fears are acknowledged and options discussed well in

---

5 Azrael is referred to in Islam as the Angel of Death, responsible for taking the souls of the deceased.

advance of any need or demand for abrupt changes that can feel devastating.

My dear father, in my remaining years, I will do everything in my power to help clients and loved ones feel better-prepared and well-informed of supportive options, so they feel empowered to make short- and long-term decisions that won't haunt them. I will make sure that our pain and sadness will not have been wasted. I will use our experience to help families advocate around advanced planning in ways that mitigate complexities of grief. Through your life and legacy, I will assist others in nurturing their loved ones more tenderly in life's most delicate moments.

Finally, daddy I will always protect mom. Your dedication to her will live on through me. I will keep my promise to always keep my eye on her for you. Through the easy times and the hard, I will have her back and work on accepting and seeing her in all of the ways that you did. I am grateful for you both. Thank you for loving us in all of the ways that you did.

Thank you for being the best father, mentor, friend, and ally I could ever have asked for. I release you with love and pray for your peace until we meet again.

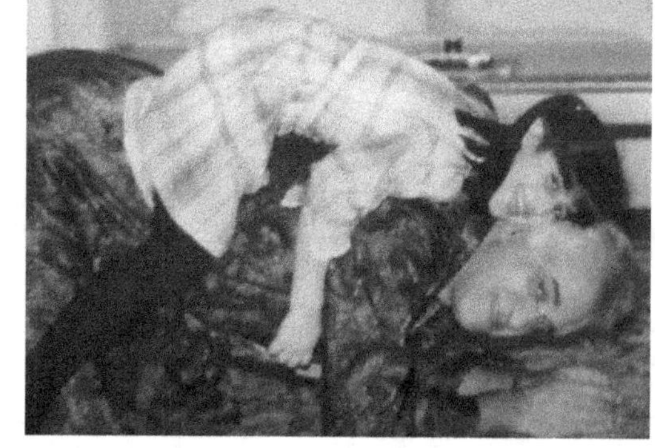

Love,
Your MonkeyFace

COMMITMENT STATEMENTS

As mentioned earlier in the text, one of the most pivotal aspects of your letter is the *commitments* section. I encourage you to continue reading it daily as a metric for future-driven choices. Writing and reading the *Release With Love Letter* once is powerful in the moment and can certainly spark insights. Continuing to read the letter and honoring the *commitments* are where profound healing and change lie. Doing so transforms your pain into purpose, renews and deepens existing relationships, and sparks more meaningful future connections.

Use your *commitments* to direct what you will make your pain mean moving forward. Below are examples of *commitments* as stand-alone readings. There is great power in revisiting your *commitment* statements for weeks and months following your letter:

Dear 28-Year Old Self,

You made me a better person by teaching me patterns I don't want to repeat. I'm sorry you had to hurt for me to learn that lesson. I will honor you and your memory by staying sober and making at least one healthy choice a day. I will honor you by remembering that it's okay to smile even after loss. I will honor you by asking for help when I need it, remembering that it's brave to ask for help. I will honor you by turning to prayer for wisdom, strength, and surrender daily.

Dear Sister,

I will honor you and your memory by exploring nature more and truly embracing life. I will go on hikes with our family and tend to the garden. I will honor you by reminding myself that hurt and loss are normal parts of life. I will remember that life goes on after pain and that it's okay to be happy, to appreciate life, and to smile even after losing someone I love. I will lead a life you'll enjoy watching from above. I will be brave and ask for help when I need it. I will keep asking until I find the support I need.

Dear Comrade,

You were one of the bravest guys I've known. It was a privilege to stand by your side. I will honor you by being outspoken in protecting those around me. I will actively listen to the pain of those around me. I will support others in need. I will pay it forward and surprise fellow veterans with generosity as a reminder of the goodness in the world around us.

I will honor the anniversary of your passing by allowing myself to feel happy. I will look for the joy and compassion that we shared! I will no longer avoid people who remind me of you. I will lean into them and consider there may be a message in those encounters. I forever celebrate our friendship. I believe you're watching from somewhere. I'm going to give you a more joyful and exciting show to watch!

Dear Self 2 Years Ago,

You made me a better person by modeling self-care and independence. I will honor you by allowing myself to have fun again! I will honor you by going to the gym at least 2-3 days/week and eating more to nourish my body. I will laugh more and leave the house at least once a day to do things I enjoy. I will honor you by doing things on my own and having fun again! I will honor you by doing more to help around the house and I will get to work on time to be the team member my coworkers deserve. I will honor you be reclaiming the parts of me that I lost.

Dear Mom,

I will honor you by focusing on the good moments—the moments when we laugh together, the efforts I see you making for us, and your smile. You have such a beautiful smile! You're funnier than I give you credit for!

Mom, I know that you have a scared little girl inside of you too. In your honor, I will ask people in my world what gives them joy, what makes them afraid, and how I can love them in ways that feel good to them. I will communicate in ways that help others around me feel safe. I will honor you by cherishing that every meal you bring me is your way of saying you adore me and want me to live a life of ease. You have a different way of showing me love, and I honor that there is still gentleness in your way. Through food, I will channel your voice that you love me. When I feel overwhelmed or unseen, I will soften my heart and remind myself of your love and intention.

Mom, I will honor our relationship by showing up for my partner when he is hurt, by honoring my commitment to partnership, and by always making sure dinner is on the table even when I don't want to. I will meet my partner at the door when he arrives home. I will speak his love language. I will resist unhelpful patterns of silence and will express my thoughts and feelings lovingly and vulnerably. I will uphold boundaries in healthy and loving ways. I will go for a walk without my phone when I feel hurt. I will lay in surrender as I breathe in beauty in moments. I will write next time I am in pain. I will uplift others and bond over peoples' gifts and strengths. In your honor, I will remain mindful of qualities I admire in each person I meet.

To My Sweet Inner Child at 6 Years Old,

You are still so innocent baby girl. You have the heart of a young child simply wanting love. When you question whether you are tainted or feel you have damaged your innocence, remember—you are not that powerful. You are still perfect in your creation and right where you are meant to be.

I will honor and protect you better by not blaming you when I get hurt, by normalizing that we all make mistakes and act from fear. I will remind you that you are not your mistakes. You are strong enough to act from love, even when you're scared of the outcome. I will remind you that others may be scared too.

I will honor you by being discerning around who is and isn't trustworthy with your feelings and your hurt. It is wonderful to be kind, but I will remind you not to give yourself away with your kindness. You are so tender yet so strong. I will guide you not to mistake attention for love. I will honor you by acting and speaking in ways I won't regret. I will recognize distress as a sign of boundaries or expectations unmet.

Baby girl, I will honor you by focusing on what I am giving rather than what I am receiving. I will reflect on what is good inside me and in others.

When hurt, I will remind myself it may be my past coming forward. I will be careful not to take that out on others. I will instead share vulnerably and allow trusted others to show up for me. I will protect my tender heart and take space as needed when I feel moments of pain. I will honor you by being kinder to gentler with myself, accepting of others, and inviting of those who've shown themselves loving and kind.

RECEIVE WITH LOVE LETTERS

Whether you're wrestling with unresolved feelings surrounding a loss or striving to maintain a healthy connection to what has been lost, the following are examples of how you might craft imagined, healthy responses to *Release With Love Letters*. Focus these letters on enduring positive legacies that persist after loss and on blessings or directions that may still be cultivated in meaningful, purpose-driven ways after loss.

Remember, mistakes do not define a person. Use pain from the past to inform lessons that can guide future decisions. Seek to find peace with unanswered questions. Extend yourself compassion around regrets, offer grace for what you (or others) may not have known before, and find comfort in knowing you can choose differently moving forward.

Dear Self,

I forgive you. I forgive you for what you did. I understand you did what you felt you had to do at that time. You were so scared for your future. What's done is done. Do not hold this against yourself. Forgive yourself before you lose yourself in the guilt. You've changed. You've learned. You've come so far. I'm here for you. Know you're not a monster. You are not a bad person. You are not your mistakes. Know that I love you. I know you feel lost. I know you feel guilty. You feel scared. I know you sometimes even hate yourself. You and I will find a way to get past this...to let it go.

I know you wanted to do the right thing back then. You just didn't know how. You didn't know then what you know now, and it hurts to live with the pain of that. I know you would make a different decision today. It's okay that you didn't know then. I'm proud of who you are today. I love you, and I'll always be here for you. We're on this journey together. I'm not going anywhere.

Dearest MonkeyFace,

Smiling when you walked into a room was easy because you were my favorite creation. You made me and your mother so proud. You made everything in life look effortless. I always loved how sensitive you are. It's one of your greatest gifts. I was just as sensitive. I just showed it differently. You were always just like me, sentimental, smart, thoughtful, and never met a stranger.

Elish, I never thought I would have children. God blessed me and your mother with you. You were always our miracle. Everything I did from the day you were born was for you and your mother...to see you both comfortable, happy, and safe. I wanted you both to have a life of ease.

Please don't feel guilty about my final years. I remember the countless hours and days you spent sitting by my side in the hospitals and final resting home. You remember I even told you that my abrupt decision to move to Arizona the day I got out of the hospital was because of the bond and time we shared when you'd visit me three times a day every day that I was in the hospital. I didn't want your mother and me to live another day of our lives away from you.

I know how hard you tried to keep my mind busy when my health deteriorated. I always knew how much you both loved me. I didn't want to forget a single moment with you and your mother. Yes, those last years were hard on everyone, but I was okay Elish. I know you saw it in the photos you took that last year. Even with all of the changes, I was still smiling in almost every picture. For someone whose general disposition was always so serious, I looked so happy in those photos you took in the last year of my life Elish. That's because I was.

Even on my most challenging days, I was so happy when I was with you and your mom, no matter what we were doing. I was always taken care of. Your mother kept me alive a good ten years past my shelf life! By the time I went, I was ready. Just like you remember, you know I was ready because I told you so. God lifted the veil of my limitations those final days to ensure you knew you were my favorite memory and proudest achievement. The day I met your mother was the best day of my life second only to the day you were born with that head full of hair! My little MonkeyFace.

Elish, I hope you'll always think of me and smile when you see the simple things I enjoyed every day of my life…red roses, climbing rose bushes, sugar cubes, tea and steak knives, ducks and lakes, Italian salad dressing, shih tzus and rugs, drafting tables, lawn mowers, poetry, feta cheese! Do you remember how I'd tease you to enjoy bread with your big chunks of feta cheese? MonkeyFace, we share a gift for seeing beauty in the mundane. Beauty and goodness are all around us.

I've always admired your ability to see the good in everyone. Never lose that. Take care of your mother for me. I visit her as often as I can in her dreams. She may not express her feelings like we did, but I sure did pick a good one, and boy, does she love you. You're her sole purpose for living. Know that I'm always watching down on you both, and I am so proud of you. I've always been proud of who you were and am even more proud of who you're becoming. I know you question that sometimes. Please don't. I couldn't be prouder to have you as my daughter. And remember, whenever you're hurting or sad, *Bozorg Mishi, Yadet Mire!*

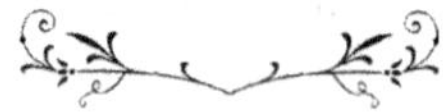

Chapter 4:

A Prayer For Those Who Have Experienced Sudden Loss

For those who have experienced a more abrupt or sudden loss, this grief can feel uniquely different, devastating, and heavy. Unexpected loss similarly comes in many forms, ranging from death, divorce, separation, and breakups to distance, religious change, identity change, sickness, trauma, a longing for a childhood or parent you wish you would have had, an estranged relationship that leaves you longing, or an unborn baby.

Sudden loss tends to feel swift, though aspects of it may still have taken place gradually over time. In the aftermath of loss, individuals may experience regret, resolve, or in some cases relief. Even so, pain often underlies them all at some stage—pain often riddled with sadness, internal conflict, or confusion.

As an added means of support and perspective, I offer a prayer that normalizes the stages of grief you may experience and provides statements of emotional validation. I hope these sentiments bring you moments of peace and a sense of feeling understood, serving as a guiding light through the grieving process. You may notice that the words of the prayer sound reminiscent of the stages of grief referenced by Kübler-Ross (1969). Please give yourself permission to feel it all.

While there is no cure for grief, there can be peace and joy after loss—these generally begin with acceptance. My hope is that your Release With Love Letter helps you move not only toward acceptance but toward seeing beauty in what lies ahead. I hope you commit to cultivating opportunities for laughter and light as you move forward.

While the author of this prayer is unknown, I hope they know how impactful their words have been to many whom they have touched. I have made slight modifications to meet clients where they are spiritually. I encourage you to substitute the greeting however you feel most aligned. For example, you might consider Dear Universe, God, Higher Power, Friend, or an alternative reference that feels most supportive and protective. May the following words validate your experience and offer you strength as you heal.

Dear Universe,

Today, I ask for the strength to let go. I know that this experience has served its purpose in my life. I know that the time has come to move forward, but I am afraid. Please give me the strength to let go.

Today, I ask for the courage to move forward. I know that there is no more I can give, nothing else I can receive by remaining where I am. I know that your divine purpose has been served and that there is something even greater waiting for me on the other side of this, but right now I am in pain. The pain that I feel keeps me stuck right where I am. Please give me the strength and the courage to move forward.

Today, I ask for the wisdom to forgive. I feel so much anger. So much shame. So much guilt. I am trying so hard to figure out what I did, what I should have done, what I should have stopped doing long before now. I know that if I could forgive myself and everyone else involved, I would be able to see beyond this anger and grief, but right now I am angry. I know it is anger that keeps me right here and feeling this way. Please give me the strength, courage, and wisdom to forgive myself; then I know I will be able to forgive everyone else.

Today, I ask for understanding. I am trying to understand, but the truth is, I don't! I am trying to see the good in this, but the truth is, I can't see it! I am trying to make sense of what is going on so that I will not continue to feel the anger or the fear. If for some reason it is not time for me to understand, please, God, just take away the pain.

Today, I ask for the humility of acceptance. I confess that I do not like what is going on. I do not understand why this is happening. I am willing to humble myself. I am willing to accept this experience, but right now I want to fight. Please humble my spirit so that I may move toward acceptance.

Today, I ask for peace. I cry out for peace! I know that the presence of peace surpasses understanding. I now ask for the comforting presence of peace to overtake the fear and anger that threaten to consume me. I know that with peace I will grow in strength and courage, and I will find myself in the midst of this loss. I now open myself to receive and experience peace in the midst of this storm. I now anchor my soul in the presence of peace. I now receive and embrace the presence of peace as the reality of this moment.

Today, I stand with strength! I move with courage! I act wisely! I am open to divine understanding! I humbly accept all of my thoughts and feelings, and I experience the presence of total peace.

For this and so much more, I am eternally grateful.

And so it is…

As we conclude this prayer for peace, let us carry its sentiments forward into the final chapter of your healing journey. In Chapter 5, 'Until We Meet Again,' I remind you of the power and influence of your healing on the world around you.

Chapter 5:
Until We Meet Again

*I*n closing, I honor your courage in taking steps to heal. Regardless of the nature of your loss or stage of your healing, there is great value in embracing the full range of your feelings. Unhealed wounds perpetuate pain. As Swiss psychiatrist and psychoanalyst Carl Jung said across his writings,

> *"Until you make the unconscious conscious, it will direct your life and you will call it fate."*

Thank you for doing your part to heal cycles of pain. As in my first book, I leave you with an excerpt from one of my favorite poems, 'Our Deepest Fear,' authored by Marianne Williamson. In part, Williamson (1992) writes:

> *There's nothing enlightened about shrinking*
> *So that other people won't feel insecure around you…*
> *We are all meant to shine…*
> *And as we let our own light shine,*
> *We unconsciously give other people permission to do the same.*
> *As we're liberated from our own fear,*
> *Our presence automatically liberates others.*

I wish you peace along your healing journey as you uncover your most tender and evolved self. As your grief lifts, I hope you may recognize the impact of your lighter footsteps on the world around you.

In my original book, *Don't Be A Stranger*, which focuses on connecting more memorably and favorably across first impressions, I asked you to consider how you would like to be remembered. I pose the same question to you now: *How would you like to be remembered? What legacy will you leave behind? How can you brighten your own path while also radiating light and kindness to those around you?*

As you heal, take your time. Heal fully. Your journey toward healing holds the power of sculpting your path forward and impacting everyone who has the privilege of crossing that path in meeting you.

May the conclusion of this book mark the beginning of your new chapter …

*"People come into your life for a **reason**, a **season** or a **lifetime**"*
(Author Unknown)

Please, treat one another honorably and live without regret…

Appendices

APPENDIX A: RELEASE WITH LOVE LETTER (With Prompts)

Dear *[name the person you are grieving]*,

What I miss about you most is …

What I regret most is …

I wish …

I remember you each time I …

[It can help keep you present in the moment if you restate name here],
You made me a better person by …

I will honor you and your memory by …
*[I refer to this as the **commitments** section wherein you identify how you will consider purposeful change in memory of that which is lost. It can help to refer back to the regrets and wish sections above to complete this. This connects your pain to purpose.]*

Thank you for being my …
[identify who the person you are grieving is to you].

I release you with love and pray for your peace …
[until we meet again…this last part can be eliminated or modified based on your belief system.]

Love,
[Your name as the person you are grieving would have known you]

APPENDIX B: RELEASE WITH LOVE LETTER (Without Prompts)

Dear …,

What I miss about you most is …
What I regret most is …
I wish …
I remember you each time I …

You made me a better person by …
I will honor you and your memory by …

Thank you for being my …
I release you with love and pray for your peace…

Love,

…

APPENDIX C: NOTE TO CLINICIANS & HELPING PROFESSIONALS

When working with clients navigating grief or seeking closure amid loss, change, or transition, I highly recommend guiding them through the *Release With Love* template in session. With your help and the structured therapeutic framework underlying this tool, clients tend to more fluidly express and explore grief-related feelings in the safe, supportive environment you create.

Your supportive role as the accountability partner guiding clients through the *Release With Love Letter* may help them more directly and willingly address unresolved emotions, confront difficult experiences, and find closure and healing. Your familiarity with their background may assist in formulating questions that prompt more reflective responses. This is more likely to enhance their journey with intentionality and self-awareness, minimizing tendencies toward avoidance or minimization.

In preparing to support clients using the *Release With Love Letter*, I recommend saving the letter template to your computer or electronic record system. This supports seamless navigation through the template whenever you anticipate a letter may facilitate emotional processing. Guide clients through the prompts in order, reading one at a time and asking that they complete the statement out loud as you type. If they become distracted or tangential, gently remind them to stay focused on the most recent prompt. Encourage authentic, specific statements to each line before moving forward.

If a client becomes angry or agitated, which is most likely during the "I miss" or "I remember" sections or when recalling past hurts or grievances, respond calmly and with a soothing tone. Invite them to join you in taking deep breaths to aid in de-escalation and refocus. Acknowledge their pain with empathy, *'I can see this is hard on you.'* Reassure them that you'll take note of their feelings and return to address them once the exercise is complete.

Emphasize the importance of remaining present, adhering to the template, and upholding a constructive focus to affect a cathartic experience.

As you proceed, continue to affirm the client's effort, acknowledging their resilience despite the emotional weight of the task. Continue to encourage mindful breathing as you revisit the pending prompt, assisting them in crafting positively-worded responses. Prompt reflection on specific experiences and identify commitments that facilitate the release of burdens they may be carrying. You and your client may be surprised to learn that once the commitment statements are written, catharsis often occurs, and revisiting hurt or anger no longer feels necessary.

Guiding Clients through the *Release With Love* Intervention

- **Establish Trust and Safety:** Create a safe, supportive, nonjudgmental space.

- **Identify the Subject of Loss:** Help identify the individual, event, or aspect to be addressed with a *Release With Love Letter*.

- **Guide the Client:** Slowly prompt the client through the structure of the *Release With Love Letter* template, encouraging elaboration if responses are brief and refocusing the client, when needed. Before reading the completed letter back to the client, ask if they recalled any details they wish to add. You as the scribe will add these to the respective section(s).

  o **Encourage your client, as needed, with prompts that help evoke depth and vulnerability, such as:**
    - *"Tell me more."*
    - *"Just a little bit more."*
    - *"Can you be a bit more specific?"*
    - *"Can you share a specific memory?"*
    - *"What do you wish were different?"*
    - *"What do you hope you'll do differently in the future?"*

- **Reflect Back:** Read the client's completed letter back to them. Allow a moment of silent reflection. Then, ask for their reactions, *'How did it feel to write that? How did it feel to hear that back?'* Process the client's reactions.

- **Closure and Release:** Before concluding, offer the client a chance to revise the letter. Then, offer to print or send them a copy using agreed-upon means. Document consent and address any privacy concerns or limitations, especially if sending files electronically. Also, suggest ways to memorialize the letter, such as performing a ritual to preserve or safely destroy it.

- **Reflect on Growth and Healing:** Ask your client about the aspects of their letter that struck them as most surprising, painful, and/or heartwarming. Use their responses to inform further clinical and supportive interventions, leveraging their reflections to steer their path toward healing and growth.

- **Follow-up and Support:** Offer ongoing support as clients continue processing their letter. Encourage daily reading initially, then periodic focus on the commitments over subsequent weeks and months. Keep record of their commitments and regularly ask about adherence for ongoing accountability. In sessions, have them read their commitments and discuss progresses made toward honoring them. Consistent follow-thru is vital for connecting their pain to purpose-driven action, enhancing self-worth and alleviating feelings of depression.

You are commended for your instrumental role in fostering a safe environment for healing. May your collaborative use of the *Release With Love Letter* serve as a catalyst for emotional healing, promoting clarity, closure, and empowerment in clients. Your dedication to helping them honor legacies, embrace acceptance, and bring the unseen to light is deeply appreciated.

APPENDIX D: GRIEF MANAGEMENT RESOURCES

The following is a list of resources you might consider connecting with or researching in your area for support in managing grief. Many can be found online and/or through local resource agencies.

- Grief counseling or therapy with professional mental health providers, therapists, grief professionals, psychologists, spiritual leaders, and others specialized in supporting individuals who are navigating the grieving process. You might find a provider through insurance, local university and community counseling centers, private practice, religious institutions, etc.

- Grief support group meetings of many kinds are often available in communities through local hospital systems, mental health centers, senior centers, Adult Day Health Care Centers, libraries, hospice agencies, etc.

- Peer Support Programs or peer-led grief support groups offer a unique format whereby those who have experienced loss lead one another in connection and support around grief resolution.

- Survivors of Suicide Group are especially helpful for those who have lost a loved one to suicide.

- Substance Abuse and Mental Health Services Administration (SAMHSA): samhsa.gov

- 988 is the three-digit number for the U.S. National Suicide Prevention Lifeline. It provides free, confidential, 24/7 support for individuals in distress, as well as resources for those concerned about someone they know. Call or text 988 to connect with a trained counselor.

- General mental health hotlines offer immediate support for those experiencing emotional distress and help individuals access resources to support managing their emotional well-being.

- American Association of Suicidology: https://suicidology.org/

- Cultural and community resources are available for those who may benefit from grief support tailored to their cultural background or community traditions.

- Community events, workshops, and seminars are often available to the public, covering topics related to emotional wellness. Search local events focusing on grief education, coping strategies, and healing activities to find opportunities for support and connection. Consider browsing event pages for local libraries, recreational or senior centers, agencies on aging or mental health, local treatment centers, among many other community resources.

- Specific resources are geared towards children and teenagers coping with grief, including children's grief support groups, books, or counseling services specializing in youth grief.

- 12-Step meetings (AA, NA, ALINON, CODA, etc. are supportive gatherings (in-person and multiple times daily online) where individuals struggling with addiction and unhealthy attachments come together to share their experiences, strengths, and hopes in a structured format. These meetings follow programming based on a twelve-step model targeting healthy recovery.

- Bereavement resources are often available through local hospital, senior center, hospice programs, and religious institutions.

- Bereavement hotlines are staffed by trained volunteers or professionals to offer emotional support, guidance, and resources to those grieving.

- Online resources, including websites, blogs, and social media groups, are dedicated to supporting individuals coping with loss. Online forums and chat support services provide a space for individuals to anonymously connect with others experiencing grief, offering an additional avenue for support.

- Educational materials including books, articles, podcasts, and videos offer information about the grieving process, coping strategies, and self-care practices. Below, find a few highly regarded books on grief recovery and the topic of detachment. Each offers insights, strategies, support, and unique perspectives for individuals navigating the complex process of grief and loss

    o "On Grief and Grieving: Finding the Meaning of Grief Through the Five Stages of Loss" by Elisabeth Kübler-Ross and David Kessler

    o "The Grief Recovery Handbook: The Action Program for Moving Beyond Death, Divorce, and Other Losses" by John W. James and Russell Friedman

    o "Grieving Mindfully: A Compassionate and Spiritual Guide to Coping with Loss" by Sameet M. Kumar

    o The Year of Magical Thinking" by Joan Didion

    o "How to Hold a Cockroach: A book for those who are free and don't know it" by Matthew Maxwell – this one is not directly related to the topic of grief, but I found it to be inspiring and uniquely helpful in addressing the topic of detachment and examining the source of grief and unresolved pain.

- Professionals are available to assist with legal and financial matters are loss that may appear daunting. These may include questions around estate planning or other practical concerns that may arise after the loss of a loved one.

- Some communities may honor ceremonies, gatherings, or traditions designed to honor and remember the deceased. This may aid in providing closure and supporting the grieving process.

- Mindful art practices combine practices of mindfulness and creative outlets involving art therapy, writing, and music as an alternative means of emotional expression.

- Engage in self-care practices can greatly support the recovery process. These may include walking and exercise, mindfulness, meditation, prayer, reading, forest bathing, spending time in nature, interacting with comforting animals, washing one's face, taking a warm shower or bath, and watching TedTalks and motivational/inspirational videos on topics that support healing.

- Consider apps that support healing and mindfulness as you embrace all feelings that arise. Apps I've greatly appreciated include *Act 10% Happier, CALM, Happify, and Insight Timer.* Clients and veterans have also found great relief with the PTSD Coach.

- If you've noticed that you've been relying on a substance for managing your pain or for symptom relief, you may benefit from additional support through apps designed to help with cessation and managing urges. Some apps you might find helpful include SMART Recovery, QuitNow!, Quit Genius, Smoke Free, Quit That!, Noom, Eat Right Now, and Rise Up + Recover. Most apps have free versions for trial. However, please use caution when choosing to ensure you are not charged if you do not wish to subscribe to paid versions.

- Finally, there are many meaningful ways to memorialize those we've lost in honorable ways. Your approach will depend on your individual preferences and the unique relationship you shared. Ideas may inform the commitment statements of your *Release With Love* Letters. Whatever you choose, make sure it feels meaningful and authentic to you. Ideas include:
    - Create a memory book or scrapbook filled with photos, letters, and mementos that remind you of your loved one.
    - Plant a tree or garden in honor of who/what is lost, or dedicate a bench, star, or plaque in a favorite park or indoor/outdoor space.

- o Make a donation to a charity or cause that was important to the departed, or establish a scholarship or fund in their memory/name.
- o Host a memorial service or gathering inviting friends and family to come together and share stories, memories, and support.
- o Create a digital memorial, such as a website, blog, or social media page, where photos, videos, and memories of the departed may be shared.
- o Volunteer your time or talents in honor of the departed. This might be through community service, mentoring, advocacy work, or with animals.
- o Keep a special object or keepsake nearby that reminds you of that which is lost, such as a piece of jewelry, clothing, photo, or a favorite book or song.
- o Create a ritual or tradition to commemorate special occasions or anniversaries, such as lighting a candle, reading a poem or letter out loud, releasing a balloon, or visiting a special place.
- o Depending on your faith, if your loved one is cremated, you might consider converting some of their ashes into 'memorial jewelry' or 'cremation crystals.' This allows individuals to keep a beautiful, tangible, and personalized memento of their loved one in view and close by.

*I'd be remiss not to recognize the wonders of modern technology.
I am grateful for OpenAI's ChatGPT (GPT-3.5), which greatly aided the final editing of this book and offered invaluable additions to referenced resources, enriching the overall content and guiding my vision to fruition.
Thank you for existing.*

APPENDIX E: RELEASE WITH LOVE (In honor of Kaylie)

I said goodbye to my perfect Kaylie on March 15, 2024, a day I will never forget. *May my perfect baby rest in peace.*

The night before I made the decision to let my baby claim her wings so she wouldn't suffer anymore, I wrote myself a Release With Love Letter. To honor my baby's legacy, I'm sharing that letter with you in the latest release of my book, launching to support your local bookstore and community. I've added a line to the original RWLL to capture one of my mother's favorite memories that she shared with me the day we said goodbye:

My dearest sweet Kaylie,

What I'll miss most about you is how your little chin would feel anytime you'd lay it on me. It's the sweetest feeling in the world, so tender yet so unquestionably powerful. I'll miss the warmth of your body every time you'd lay on me.

Baby, I regret how uncomfortable you seem. I don't think I have regrets about our life. There are plenty of what-ifs, but I remind myself of reality, that you lived a full, happy, healthy life and that we adored each other every moment of every day. I made no decision with you lightly. We have been perfect for each other. There are many times I could've been a better mother to you, but there's no way you would be as amazing as you are if we didn't work together as well as we do. You've been my companion, my cuddle buddy, and my source of peace for so many years. I only regret that I don't know how to do right by you now. I don't want to rob you of a single day that you deserve. It's so hard coming home and watching you try to fight for normalcy.

I wish I knew the right thing to do. I wish when your time came you would just slip away peacefully in your sleep so that there would be no decision to be made. I wish you looked like you were just at peace, yet I can see the pain all over you as you try to be strong for us. I will always remember you every time I see a dog, when I look at my bed, when I lay on my sofa, when I sit cross-legged in my office chair, and when I walk through my garage to the kitchen. God, you loved eating so much, just like your mama and grandpa. I will never feel the same without you on my lap.

I will always think of you when I look at my mother. You really wiggled your way into her heart. Thank you for softening her and for bringing us closer. You've even left us with jokes! She said she'll most miss how you would always wipe your cute little paws on the doormat each time you'd enter her home. We have no idea where you learned to do that! I love you so much.

Kaylie, you made me a better person by bringing out a more nurturing side in me and proving that I am absolutely capable of staying by the side of someone I love until they take their last breath. You have made me a better person by reminding me to be gracious and patient, especially during hard times. I was never upset with you when you got sick or ornery. I knew it wasn't your fault and that something was off. I knew you weren't feeling well and needed compassion. I know that when you're not yourself, you don't feel good and don't want to be that way. You're a reminder to consider best intentions and a call for love.

My little baby, I will honor you by treating people with the same tenderness I show you. I will look into their eyes the way I do yours. I will slow down and think about what they might be needing when I or they feel frustrated or scared. I will remember that it's not their fault when they don't know how to ask for what they need in a way that I can understand. I will do my best to understand. I love you so much. You are everything that is good about me, and you bring out the best in me always. I'm so sorry that we had to see these hard days together. Life with you is worth every minute.

Thank you for being my best friend and my sweet companion in life for 16 years. Thank you for holding on as long as you did and for staying happy and healthy for so much of our life together. I love you forever. There will never be another dog like you. I pray for your peace and for gentleness until we meet again, my sweet baby.

Love,
Mama

References

Barks, C. (trans.). (1995). *The Essential Rumi*. HarperOne.

Foundation for Inner Peace. (1976). A Course in Miracles. New York, NY: Viking Press.

Frankl, V. E. (1984). Man's search for meaning. Beacon Press.

Kübler-Ross, E. (1969). On death and dying. New York, NY: Scribner.

McCaine, J. H. (2022). Moments of Truth: The discovery and restoration of selfhood. Dr Jon H. McCaine Publications.

Verny, T.R. (2023, August 22). Intuition: What It Is and How It Works. *Psychology Today*.
https://www.psychologytoday.com/us/blog/explorations-of-the-mind/202308/intuition-what-it-is-and-how-it-works

Williamson, M. (1992). A Return to Love: Reflections on the Principles of "A Course in Miracles." HarperCollins.

Acknowledgments

I feel indebted to my courageous clients and loved ones who allowed me to step into the darkness with them as we navigated the path back into the light. Your willingness to share parts of your journeys to help others in their healing is admirable and awe-inspiring.

I again thank my pup-child Kalyx for the countless hours she has spent on my lap as I've written, read, and brainstormed—especially since working full-time from home. I cherish every moment with you, my little baby, and I actively seek opportunities to commemorate and crystallize as many memories with you as possible. Thank you for being my little confidante.

I don't know where I'd be without the love of my best friend and Rodan and Fields business partner, Brooke Fremouw. Brookie, you continue to carry on my father's torch. I only wish he could have met you. He would have loved what you bring out in me. You emanate the quote about surrounding yourself with people who help you fall in love with yourself when you're around them! You are the wind beneath my wings. You remind me of my strength when I feel weak. You never stop believing in me. Thank you for being the best part of me! You are a constant example of grace and compassion. You are a reminder of carrying oneself with integrity and walking without regret. Thank you for being the sister I never had, my best friend and favorite person in the world, my surrogate for everything that ever feels missing, and my partner in the business that has changed my life…first by bringing you to me! I love sharing every aspect of life with you!

To my dear friends, Cindy Wolf, Stephanie Morin, and Brookie, thank you for your willingness, without hesitation, to be my readers and editors for this text. I admire and so value your wisdom, insights, and authenticity in lovingly delivering feedback to minimize the rambling redundancies as I prepared this book. I learn so much from each of you. With your tender touches, this manuscript will be better positioned to help others. I am blessed to know you and to call you all my friends and influencers. You each inspire me in unique and lasting ways! And Gina Bean Monteiro, you continue to be a beacon of wisdom, kindness, light, and courage, inspiring me to believe in myself and publish content. Thank you for simply being you and for the gifts you bring to my life even when you may not realize it! Thank goodness for that not-so random meeting in Florida all those yeas ago! You are a true example of the profound impact strangers can have on each other's lives!

I also wish to extend my heartfelt thanks to Osamudiamenabdu, my dedicated editor and friend, who so patiently and supportively assisted me through the editing process for my books in the ***Don't Be A Stranger*** series. I would recommend him without hesitation to anyone undertaking a publication.

To my dearest mother, I know we both at times feel lost without Daddy. Thank you for choosing the best father a girl could ask for. Thank you for choosing to love me every day, both when it's easy and especially when it's hard. Thank you for the gift of your vulnerability for this book. Talking about feelings has always been hard for you. To know you gifted me and the world with your own *Release With Love Letters* for the publication of this book is beyond my wildest dreams. Thank you for doing what you can to fill Daddy's very big shoes so that life doesn't feel as empty without

him. Thank you for always believing in me and supporting my crazy endeavors. I love you to the moon and back.

To my dear daddy, no more words… you know. You are ever-present in my heart and in every breath I take. I love you forever! Thank you for forever lighting my path. Because of you, I know what it means to walk in the light.

About the Author

r. Nademin holds the distinction of first female board-certified psychologist in behavioral and cognitive psychology in Arizona. She serves veterans full-time as a telehealth psychologist in a large healthcare system while also supporting underserved in small, rural communities. She maintains a part-time private practice, and lectures periodically in the community on topics of professionalism, behavioral medicine, diversity, impression management, and interpersonal connection.

Dr. Nademin's contributions extend beyond clinical practice. She has been instrumental in standard-setting and curriculum development for communication, interpersonal skills, and behavioral medicine for students of osteopathic medicine. She has assumed statewide and national leadership roles, including service as Arizona Early Career Psychologist Ambassador to the American Board of Professional Psychology. She has led diversity advocacy efforts and volunteers regularly in the community.

In addition to her work in mental health and authorship, Dr. Nademin channels her entrepreneurial spirit as a Rodan + Fields Affiliate, guiding teams of empowered business owners in the anti-aging e-commerce marketplace. Those who have supported her Rodan + Fields business are the reason she is active on public platforms, sharing her journey and experiences, and the #1 reason she developed the courage to publish the *Don't Be A Stranger* series.

Dr. Nademin derives joy in watching people dream bigger as they grow in confidence, leadership skills, and investment in themselves and the community at large. She shares her expertise through education, shining a light on the beauty that surrounds us. She highlights inner and outer beauty and relishes in managing her business while traveling, bantering with strangers and helping the unseen feel seen.

Dr. Nademin values creativity and curiosity, and her business constantly challenges her outside of her comfort zone, compelling her to find unique and unexpected approaches to excellence in an ever-changing industry. She delights in seeing people take control of the aging process by investing in self-care with high-quality skin and hair care products and fostering meaningful business partnerships. She feels most energized by empowering others to lead, inspire, and positively impact the lives of others. Even when faced with adversity, she remains steadfast in modeling grit and perseverance.

In her leisure time, Dr. Nademin treasures moments spent with her friends and mother or curled up on the couch indulging in favorite shows with her dog Kaylie. She draws inspiration from travel and loves watching people express their passions, whether through breakdancing, stand-up comedy, open mics, or spoken word performances. Dr. Nademin regularly volunteers for local charities, where she revels in meeting others who share a commitment to giving back.

In her respective roles, Dr. Nademin finds fulfillment in making a positive impact on others. She is especially passionate about encouraging diversification in talents and income streams, all while maintaining a steadfast commitment to serving others. For more about Dr. Nademin, please subscribe to her YouTube channel and follow her on social media using the handles below:

YouTube: https://www.youtube.com/@elicianademinnuggetsofwisdom
Facebook (https://www.facebook.com/elicianademin)
Instagram (https://www.instagram.com/dreambiggerwithelicia)

To support Dr. Nademin's efforts to shine her light on a global platform, consider supporting her Rodan and Fields endeavors. Through her R+F venture, she has expanded her mostly private impact, shifting from individual sessions, one client, one hour at a time, to engaging on a larger, public scale, touching lives for even brief moments every day! This expansion has been made possible solely thanks to the generosity of strangers and friends who have supported her in business and believed in her potential.

Dr. Nademin loves to offer free skin and hair care consultations to educate others on safe and effective products for optimal skin and hair health. The most impactful way to support her mission of spreading goodness is by taking her free online consultation at the link below and ordering products that help *you* feel your best. The online assessment, developed by world-renowned, board-certified Dermatologists, Doctors Rodan and Fields, integrates artificial intelligence to personalize your results. Trusting Dr. Nademin in selecting products that help you feel most confident, healthy, and radiant is the ultimate compliment.

Another meaningful way to align with Dr. Nademin's vision of promoting self-care and investing in others is by sharing her links and contributing the cost of self-care products to be donated to a charity or business of your choice. To explore this option further, please contact Dr. Nademin at elician@gmail.com.

Please take advantage of the free online consultation at the link below:

https://4anewyou.myrandf.com/en-us/solution-tool

May you feel and become your best in the days ahead. May your journey be illuminated with light and love present in moments every day.

Dr. Nademin's certifications, licenses, and experience in Psychology have no connection to her consulting, marketing, or skincare business. Neither respective area gives her special expertise in another or serve as therapy or clinical care.

"Grief is in two parts. The first is loss.
The second is the remaking of life."[6]

-Anne Roiphe

---

⁶ This quote drawn from the book Epilogue; A Memoir, published by American writer and journalist Anne Roiphe in 2008.

Notes and Reflections

Remember to reference all RWLL core elements:

What you will most miss / Regret / Wish / Remember / What makes you better / What you will honor / Gratitude

Notes and Reflections

Remember to reference all RWLL core elements:

*What you will most miss / Regret / Wish / Remember / What makes you better /
What you will honor / Gratitude*

Notes and Reflections

Remember to reference all RWLL core elements:

*What you will most miss / Regret / Wish / Remember / What makes you better /
What you will honor / Gratitude*

Notes and Reflections

Remember to reference all RWLL core elements:

What you will most miss / Regret / Wish / Remember / What makes you better / What you will honor / Gratitude